$3,00

GERANIUMS FOR HOME AND GARDEN

GERANIUMS
For Home and Garden

ALAN SHELLARD

David & Charles
Newton Abbot   London   North Pomfret (Vt)

British Library Cataloguing in Publication Data

Shellard, Alan
  Geraniums for home and garden.
  1. Geraniums
  I. Title
  635.9′33′216   SB413.G3

ISBN 0-7153-8124-5

Library of Congress Catalog Card Number 81-67004

Typeset and printed in Great Britain
by Butler & Tanner Ltd, Frome and London
for David & Charles (Publishers) Limited
Brunel House Newton Abbot Devon

Published in the United States of America
by David & Charles Inc
North Pomfret Vermont 05053 USA

Contents

Introduction

This book is about *pelargoniums*—but as most people know these plants as 'geraniums', that is what the title has to be.

I might welcome the time when everyone recognizes my favourite plants as pelargoniums, but I'm certain this won't happen before I have repotted my final plant—and I'm nowhere near through my three score years and ten yet. When my wife can confidently ask the greengrocer for '5 lb of *Solanum tuberosum var.* King Edward' to provide the basic material for my chips, then perhaps such a book as this could be correctly titled.

Meanwhile the knowledgeable and expert reader will, if regretfully, have recognized common usage when picking up the book; and the non-expert reader will cheerfully continue, as I do, to refer to these plants as geraniums—if only so that friends know what he or she is talking about.

My years spent in growing geraniums have been considerably enhanced by the writings of other people, and if interest in and knowledge of these marvellous plants are to be sustained, so too should the flow of literature. The explanations and advice on cultivation that follow must result from a conglomeration of personal experiences and advice from my betters, accumulated over the years. But I also have a more specific reason for writing this book.

For many years now I have been fortunate enough to have the job of compiling the annual Top Ten lists of the various classes of geraniums on behalf of the British & European Geranium Society, to whom I am indebted for permission to use the results. This work has brought me into contact annually with fifty or so respected amateur enthusiasts throughout Britain, whose combined opinions of countless varieties go to make up the lists. So I can confidently refer to 'popular modern geraniums' knowing that I am supported by the overall opinion of many of Britain's leading amateur growers, to whom I am also indebted.

All the varieties (more correctly 'cultivars') described have proved their worth to many top growers in recent years (the 1970s) and are 'modern' in that respect only. Some have been with us for a century while others have swept to popularity in the past few years.

And although I'm principally intending to discuss the basics of good geranium growing with the new or recent enthusiast in mind, I hope there will be sufficient to interest the more experienced so that they will make this an acceptable addition to their bookshelves.

One of the problems I anticipate is that, like humans, the geranium is a natural individual; so variations and exceptions that apply within virtually every group or classification render it difficult to make general statements with total conviction. Personally, I find this individuality to be perhaps the most appealing, interesting, challenging—call it what you will—characteristic of the geranium.

However, it does mean that actual experience in growing particular varieties in your own personal environment will ultimately prove of greater value to those who seek perfection than the, necessarily, basic principles and guidelines discussed in general terms within the book.

If the following pages should prove of sufficient interest and value to tempt the reader to explore the full range of types of geraniums mentioned, I'll be delighted—and so will you!

1 The Range of Geraniums

This chapter is the most technical and ideally perhaps would be better 'slipped in' after interest has been stimulated. That, however, would very much put the cart before the horse and if readers can be persuaded to take the medicine immediately I promise it will quickly get better.

The pelargonium is a member of the Geraniaceae family (there is another explanation of the common name geranium) and a more confusing family it is difficult to imagine. The name derives from the Greek word *geranos*, meaning crane, and presumably refers to the similarity between that bird's beak and the seed fruit of all Geraniaceae. In addition to the hardy geranium (the wild 'cranesbill' will be a familiar plant to many Britons), two other principal genera of the family are pelargonium ('storksbill') and erodium ('heronsbill'). While ornithologists and botanists may be able to differentiate between the beaks of these birds and the numerous genera and sub-genera of the geranium family respectively, the differences will be of little consequence to most 'geranium' growers.

Botanically, it is probably more than sufficient, even for the enthusiast, to know that the flowers of geraniums are invariably regular with six or more stamens. Pelargoniums, on the other hand, have no more than five stamens, irregular petals (before hybridization took a hand), and a tube for nectar as part of the floret stem which is not found in the true geranium.

The pelargonium is generally native to South Africa, particularly the Cape area, although a few have been found elsewhere from Australia to Tristan da Cunha. Generally, however, its natural environment is arid desert, which doubtless accounts for its remarkable tolerance of lack of attention.

The cultivated varieties (hence 'cultivar') with which this book is principally concerned are plants that have been created by, generally, deliberate and continual cross-breeding between pelargonium species and the resulting progeny. These differ

Fig. 1 (a classification chart for Pelargonium/Geranium types)

FLOWER	ZONAL BASIC GREEN	ZONAL BASIC GOLD	ZONAL BASIC BICOLOUR	ZONAL BASIC TRICOLOUR	ZONAL DWARF GREEN	ZONAL DWARF GOLD	ZONAL DWARF BICOLOUR	ZONAL DWARF TRICOLOUR	ZONAL MINIATURE GREEN	ZONAL MINIATURE GOLD	ZONAL MINIATURE BICOLOUR	ZONAL MINIATURE TRICOLOUR	REGAL BASIC GREEN	REGAL BASIC BICOLOUR	REGAL DWARF GREEN	IVY-LEAVED BASIC GREEN	IVY-LEAVED BASIC BICOLOUR	IVY-LEAVED DWARF GREEN	HYBRID IVY BASIC GREEN	HYBRID IVY BASIC BICOLOUR	OTHERS
SINGLE	1 o	5 o	7 o	9 o	11 o	14 •	16 •	19 •	21 o	23 o	24 o	25 o	26 o	28 •	29 o	30 o	33 •	35 •	38 •		41 SPECIES •
SEMI DOUBLE & DOUBLE	2 o	6 o	8 •	10 •	12 o	15 o	17 •	20 •	22 o				27 •			31 o	34 •	36 o	39 o	40 •	42 PRIMARY HYBRIDS
																					43 HYBRIDS
ROSETTE & ROSEBUD	3 •						18 •									32 •		37 •			44 SCENTED LEAVES
CACTUS	4 o				13 o																45 UNIQUES

o Many varieties available   • Few varieties available

Examples: 1 Kathleen Gamble, 2 Regina, 3 Appleblossom Rosebud, 4 Noel, 5 Mrs Quilter, 6 Ursula Key, 7 Mrs Mappin, 8 Mrs Parker, 9 Henry Cox, 10 Golden Brilliantissima, 11 Dwarf Miriam Basey, 12 Deacon Lilac Mist, 13 Tangerine, 14 Golden Hieover, 15 Morval, 16 Frank Headley, 17 Madame Butterfly, 18 Spitfire, 19 Miss Burdette Coutts, 20 Hurdy Gurdy, 21 Grace Wells, 22 Jane Eyre, 23 Lisa, 24 Silver Kewense, 25 Gwen, 26 Aztec, 27 Phyllis Richardson, 28 Miss Australia, 29 Catford Belle, 30 Butterflies, 31 Ailsa Garland, 32 Beatrice Cottington, 33 L'Elegante, 34 Duke of Edinburgh, 35 Jeanne d'Arc, 36 Sugar Baby, 37 Eulalia, 38 Cheshire Gem, 39 Millfield Gem, 40 Elsi, 41 P. *Graveolens*, 42 P × *kewense*, 43 Little Gem, 44 Mabel Grey, 45 Madame Nonin

from Nature's own hybridizations only in that the latter have seldom been subjected to the same intense cross-breeding and are always referred to in Latin terms and called varieties (var.) to indicate that they originated in the wild.

Several attempts to classify the geraniums we now grow have been put forward which have and will continue to serve geranium enthusiasts well. The new grower may appreciate the table (page 10) which sets out the total current alternatives (classifications), given the restricted criteria currently used for classifying geraniums.

The table uses a principal division each of which is theoretically capable of three further progressive subdivisions. Mercifully, the 156 potential classifications have not been achieved in practice and indeed may not be achievable. In the case of a subdivision which has apparently not (yet) evolved, that section is omitted from the table, whereas classifications with very few known cultivars are marked with a black dot. As will be seen, this still leaves a few specific types that are best described as self-classifying and that if subdivided would not follow the divisions normally applied to the cultivated varieties.

The principal divisions used are the 'types', which for this purpose can be restricted to zonals, regals, ivy-leaved and hybrid ivy, all of which are described more fully in subsequent chapters.

The subdivisions could have been used in any order but, for the purpose of the table, the plant 'habit' or normal growth characteristic has been used initially. In accordance with current practice, these are shown as miniature, dwarf and basic, although the latter could equally well be termed 'usual' or 'normal' (but not 'standard', as this might be confused with the single-upright-stem method of cultivation). Obviously, such a subdivision is suspect, as unlike the others it is imposed by humans and is not a matter of fact but of opinion; and indeed even this division is itself capable of further subdivision into at least large, average and small; but where would it end and what would be gained? In fact this subdivision is acceptable or necessary only for the convenience of the modern geranium grower as a result of the many cultivars raised specifically as dwarfs or miniatures, particularly among the zonals.

The second subdivision relates to the colour of the foliage. In the case of zonals the permutations, if not endless, are certainly numerous, with various shades of green (including the almost black), with or without zone, or with two or more shades of green, all available within the general heading 'green'; similarly for 'gold' which is intended to accommodate the leaf colourings between yellow and bronze.

The 'bicolour' heading is generally accepted as applying to green and white or green and cream leaves with or without a zone overlying the green portion.

The 'tricolours', which appear only among the zonals, are generally green with yellow/gold or silver/white/cream edges or markings, and in this section only is the zone essential, as it is this, overlying both the other colours, which creates the multicoloured variations for which these plants are justifiably popular. A few bicolours have appeared in the regal and ivy-leaved sections, but as yet they are of little consequence in the regals and several of the so-called bicolour ivies have little more than white or cream veins in their leaves and are not truly bicoloured, however attractive they look.

Three descriptions that have been deliberately avoided are variegated, ornamental and fancy-leaved—often applied to bi-colour and tricolour-leaved cultivars and sometimes even to golden-leaved. These terms can be so widely interpreted as to mean all things to all men, particularly when considering any zonal cultivar with a pronounced and distinctive zone. The more specific descriptions used appear preferable, even if 'green', 'gold' and 'bicolour' would each be more correct if the words 'with or without zonal markings' were added.

The final subdivision deals with the formation of the indivi-dual florets which go to make up the flowerhead. The sections are:

Single-flowered—each floret normally having five petals.
Semi-double flowered—each floret normally having more than five petals but with similar form to single-flowered, the extra petals being few in number and usually uneven, distorted, curled or quilled.
Double-flowered—each floret having more than five petals, the additional petals normally being five or more in number of good shape and more uniformly distributed than semi-doubles, but seldom opening fully, thereby giv-ing a depth to the floret.

Semi-double and double are generally grouped together, perhaps because the dividing line between the two is so difficult to establish.

Rosette-flowered—each floret having considerably more than five petals so as to reduce the size of the floret and alter the more usual shape.
Rosebud-flowered—as for rosette, but the centre petals remain tight in the centre giving the appearance of a very small rosebud just beginning to open.

Here again, rosette-flowered and rosebud-flowered can be grouped together, the former being normally applied to ivy-leaved cultivars and the latter to a small group of basic zonals.

Cactus-flowered—florets consist of furled or quill-shaped petals, the number in each floret depending on the cultivar.

One could impose further subdivisions to accommodate existing cultivars which, while already falling into a classification, nevertheless form a distinct subsection within that classification. An example of this that is genetically sound would be to subdivide at least the various zonal classifications when necessary into 'diploids' and 'tetraploids', referring to the plants' chromosome count, which in turn imparts a different appearance and growing habit.

The man-made divisions of dwarf and miniature, and thereby basic, not unnaturally create their own problems—for example, when is a small dwarf a large miniature? This must remain a matter of personal opinion based on the particular method of growing selected, but when a cultivar has large flowers but is in all other respects a miniature, or conversely has minute flowers on an otherwise basic-sized plant, you do feel in need of a qualifying term.

If the term 'Novelty' were to be applied to cultivars naturally falling within a particular classification but which had one or more characteristic out of keeping with that classification, then the whole purpose of classification—to communicate a description with uniform and acceptable brevity—begins to become attainable. A recent attractive introduction from America called 'Celebration' might therefore be described as a 'Tetraploid—(Large Flower) Novelty—Double (Flowered)—Green (Leaved)—Dwarf—Zonal—Geranium' by one experienced

13

enthusiast to another, and by dropping each leading subdivision in turn, depending on the knowledge and experience of his audience, he could reduce the description to 'Dwarf Zonal Geranium' to a new geranium grower or even 'Geranium' to his non-gardening and perhaps uninterested workmates. Such is the art of communication and the advantage of uniform classification.

The other specific classifications, species, primary hybrids, scented and uniques will be dealt with later.

THE MANY USES OF GERANIUMS
It's not surprising that so varied a range of plants as those in the geranium family have a very wide range of uses. Undoubtedly, the geranium today is popular mainly for its general decorative effect as a complete plant, although the situations in which this effect can be utilized are numerous.

There is one obvious restriction—the plant must have a frost-free environment. Unless all plants are bought each year, which would eliminate many of the pleasures and advantages of growing geraniums, you must be able to provide some form of winter protection in those regions of the world that enjoy, or suffer, sub-zero (0°C) temperatures. Such protection does not have to be a heated greenhouse, although that is the ideal, but can be any situation expected to remain at above freezing temperature. Even a box under the spare bed has been known to provide a home where plants can survive the winter, although they are unlikely actually to flourish during the time they spend there!

In Britain, thanks to our generally excellent municipal parks departments as well as individual gardeners, the geranium remains one of the most widely used annual bedding plants. Some of the formal bedding schemes (including the famous Buckingham Palace beds of red geraniums) could surely not be bettered over the five or so months that they are in bloom. The fact that many of these are now F1 hybrids is more a matter of economics, in that large organizations find it less expensive to grow annually from seed, than an implied criticism of the previously grown named varieties.

Informal beds, whether of mixed varieties of geraniums or of geraniums interspersed with other plants, are more the prerogative of individual gardeners. Apart from the very obvious advantage of the long flowering period, giving summer and autumn colour in the garden, they require a minimum of attention once established. Informal beds of individual 'spot plants' also provide an ideal way for the greenhouse geranium grower to use up his previous year's overwintered plants and maintain stock of particular varieties.

There are many other outdoor uses for the geranium which, as an all-rounder, compares favourably with almost any other plant. Hanging baskets and wall baskets are ideal for ivy-leaved varieties, as are ornamental walls and window boxes, particularly if zonal varieties are mixed in. Troughs, urns or other garden containers provide suitable growing conditions for all geraniums.

While most geraniums perform very pleasingly in semi-shade, they give of their best in situations that enjoy maximum sunshine. If kept down to a reasonable height, they withstand winds better than most annuals.

The 1960s and 1970s saw a great improvement in dwarf and miniature zonal varieties, suitable for even the narrower indoor window-sills of modern homes. Geraniums delight in full light and do not perform too well away from windows, but even north-facing windows are quite suitable—positively preferable in the case of regals in flower. Unless double-glazing is fitted, plants should be moved further back into the room every evening and replaced every morning during the winter, until the fear of frosts has passed.

Many types and varieties are obviously well suited by the conditions available in most homes although, like many other houseplants, they perform better in rooms not directly heated by gas fires. A worthwhile type of plant to keep around the house is one with a strongly scented leaf, such as *P. graveolens*. This type, while principally grown for its foliage rather than its flowers, is a most effective room-freshener, quite capable of disposing overnight of the drinking-and-smoking stuffiness that otherwise still lingers in a room next morning.

Greenhouses are, and will probably remain, the most suitable environment in which to grow individual plants in pots. During the summer months at least you can equally well use such structures as an unheated glass or polythene lean-to, a garden frame or any construction giving maximum light and sufficient protection from wind and rain. Certainly, almost every specimen geranium plant that is exhibited or displayed at the numerous flower shows that abound in Britain from late spring to early autumn will have been grown in a greenhouse or similar situation. Virtually every geranium that is bought in Britain, whether as a pot plant or a bedder, fully grown or no more than a rooted cutting, will have been produced in a greenhouse. Bedding plants from a reliable source should have been hardened off in an open frame for a couple of weeks, but it is always advisable to repeat this process yourself before planting out into the open.

Many geraniums available today are suitable for use as cut flowers in single buttonholes or massed bowls. Geranium flowers and foliage are frequently found within flower arrangements, from the smallest corsage to large majestic arrangements at flower shows or in churches. Tricolour and bicolour zonal and bicolour ivy-leaved geranium foliage plants are always popular with flower arrangers as well as the regal and basic zonal plants grown for their flowers.

There are even some cooking recipes which call for a few of the scented leaves from geraniums, and at least one home-made wine can apparently be produced from the leaves of *P. radens* ('Radula'). Dried, scented leaves from geraniums can also be used in a pot-pourri or the small scented bags for drawers and linen-cupboards.

Finally, there is no doubt that geraniums have been used as, or in the manufacture of, cosmetics for a very long time, and they were attributed with medicinal properties in earlier times. Which just goes to show what a talented plant the geranium is!

'Frank Headley', an excellent all-round, bicolour-leaved (green and white), single-flowered zonal, showing the partially primitive petal formation. This is the most popular greenhouse bicolour *(Pat Brindley)*

'Crystal Palace Gem', an interesting variety whose ornamental light-yellow leaves have an inconsistent and irregular butterfly marking of a much darker green. A poor flowerer, grown principally for its foliage *(Garden News)*

2 Growing Habit and Propagation

A little knowledge may well be a dangerous thing with geraniums, as the multitude of types, and of variations within those types, creates a situation in which even 'basic' facts could require lengthy qualifications and listing of exceptions. Nevertheless, it is obvious that without acquiring a limited level of knowledge initially, it is impossible to develop a more detailed understanding of any subject whether by experience or discussion. This multiplicity of variations makes the accumulation of further knowledge by practical growing deeply absorbing and interesting, and it soon becomes obvious that, as with so many things in life, the more one knows about geraniums the more there is to know.

Zonal geraniums are undoubtedly the largest group, both by types and in the number of cultivars, so that they must assume the principal position in general discussion, with apologies to the regal and ivy-leaved enthusiasts.

The growing habit of zonal geraniums is principally as shown on page 20. Before preparing itself for flowering the stem generally develops with single leaves on alternate sides. As it reaches the flowering period a flower bud develops opposite one of the leaves. As this occurs a side shoot generally begins to grow from the leaf joint immediately below the flower bud, and this shoot first develops a double leaf joint, the two leaves being on opposite sides of the new stem, before reverting to the usual style of growing single alternate leaves up to the flowering stage.

The leaf joint that follows above the flower bud will normally develop as a double leaf joint also, and these leaves are not directly in line with previous leaves but at an angle to them. In the more floriferous, and therefore more popular, varieties the next leaf joint will again be a single leaf and flower bud. The stem and side shoots will continue to develop in this way until

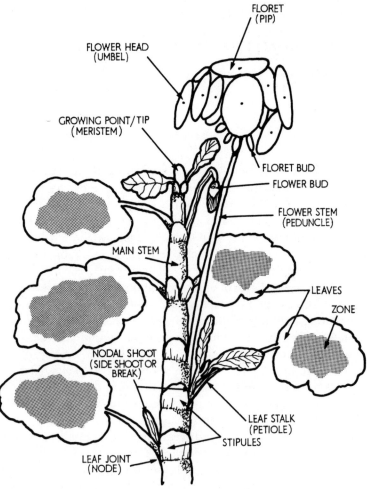

FLORET
(PIP)

FLOWER HEAD
(UMBEL)

GROWING POINT/TIP
(MERISTEM)

FLORET BUD

FLOWER BUD

FLOWER STEM
(PEDUNCLE)

MAIN STEM

LEAVES

ZONE

NODAL SHOOT
(SIDE SHOOT OR
BREAK)

LEAF STALK
(PETIOLE)

STIPULES

LEAF JOINT
(NODE)

Fig. 2   The makings of a geranium

growing conditions become unfavourable, when growth reverts
to single leaf joints without flower buds.

As each joint develops it is protected by thin leafy shields, two
to each single leaf, whether with or without a flower bud, and
three protecting each double leaf joint (four in the case of
regals). These protective shields are called stipules. At their
earliest appearance although minute they totally encompass the
following leaf joint, leaves and all. Even at this early stage,
however, the protected leaf and flower bud are always perfectly
formed. As they grow and enlarge the stipules part to allow

them to grow away and at this point the following stipules will just be apparent, no larger than a pinhead in size.

When the flower bud first appears it will be crooked like a walking stick, with the part that will form the flowerhead hanging downwards. The flower stem generally grows on in this form until it appears above the surrounding foliage, when it will gradually straighten the 'neck' until the first floret buds to develop can be seen pointing upwards. The complete flowerhead and each individual floret will have had their own stipulelike protection during this development and only as the earliest florets point upwards will the petals themselves begin to break through their individual protection as small splashes of colour.

The floret stems will be lengthening at this time as the petals themselves begin to unfurl. The first floret will open facing directly upwards and within a few days will have been joined by others adopting the most upright position allowed by the neighbouring florets. The florets will continue in this way; each day brings more florets, producing with luck a well-formed flowerhead. In varieties with sufficient individual florets, a complete ball of flower can be formed.

Of the various exceptions possible, perhaps the two most common among zonals are, firstly, that some varieties are reluctant to develop the side shoot at the node beneath the first (and subsequent) flowerhead; and secondly, that a few varieties will produce a flowerhead from the double leaf joint following the first flowerhead—this, of course, produces a flowerhead at three successive leaf joints and creates a very floriferous effect for a short period.

Ivy-leaved geraniums show the second exception above far more frequently than do zonals, and some even continue with flowerheads at every leaf joint beyond the first flush of flowers. The ivy-leaved type also has considerably fewer florets in each flowerhead than zonals, usually between five and ten so that the complete ball shape is seldom obtained.

Since the end of the Second World War, regal varieties have been introduced which follow the growing pattern described for the zonal far more closely than older varieties did, and these have been described as 'perpetual (or continuous) flowering'. While this obviously overstates their prowess, it is nevertheless an acceptable term to differentiate between them and the still more common regal varieties that flower in flushes. In those with this more familiar habit the main stem peters out after two or three quickly produced flowerheads but, as if in compensation, about three side shoots develop from the leaf joints below the first flower and very quickly produce flowers before themselves petering out. This produces a magnificent covering of bloom that can last as long as eight weeks but appears to so exhaust the plant that it takes a couple of months' recuperation before further side shoots have developed. The blooms from these side shoots are seldom as abundant as the first flush, although very acceptable.

One of the reasons for the magnificence of a regal in full flower is the larger size of the bell-shaped florets that form the flowerhead. Though there are seldom more than six florets, each flowerhead can be as large as a basic zonal, and as they are generally much shorter-stemmed they are closer together, producing an overall covering which, in a well-grown plant, can virtually obscure the foliage.

Both regal and ivy-leaved types have different leaves from those of the zonal, but these and other differences will be described more fully in subsequent chapters.

PROPAGATION FROM CUTTINGS

The beginning for virtually all geranium varieties is a seed. Apart from some species and F1 hybrids however, the way to increase or replace your existing stock of a particular plant is vegetatively, by cuttings.

Layering (pinning a branch to surrounding soil while still attached to the parent plant so that it is sustained while it forms new roots and is only then separated from the parent), aerial rooting (partially severing a branch and enclosing the wound in an airtight polythene 'bag' containing moist peat or soilless compost so that it again forms roots before it is removed from the parent plant) and meristem culture for those with laboratory conditions, are alternatives. These however, are merely variations of the normal method of taking cuttings which, in the ordinary home or garden, remains the simplest and most successful way of making more plants from those you have.

Most geranium plants that have been grown in a container will be past their best after twelve to eighteen months and all should be replenished after twenty-four to thirty months if quality and vigour are not to suffer. There is no reason to try

22

to keep a plant longer than this as the amount of material available to produce cuttings on any mature plant is plentiful, and the success rate so high that the problem for beginners is usually a surfeit of opportunity which they find hard to resist.

When taking cuttings the object is to remove part of a mature plant without causing any ill effect to the plant or the part removed (the cutting), so that both will grow on in a healthy condition. The first essential to attain this objective is a very sharp knife or safety razor blade which will glide easily through the stem of the plant without bruising, tearing or leaving jagged edges. Ideally the blade should be sterilized between each cut, but in practice very few amateurs adopt this precaution and indeed many cuttings are removed with the nails of thumb and forefinger or with blunt penknives or secateurs, without too much harm (if any) to either plant or cutting; which merely reaffirms the tolerance of the geranium. Such deviations from the ideal are not recommended and whenever possible the following procedures should be followed for maximum success, using a sharp blade and sterilizing it as often as possible.

The cutting should be about 3 inches long, or less, for basic type plants and proportionately shorter for dwarf and miniature varieties, but that length should carry at least three leaf joints for best results. Cut the parent plant immediately above a leaf joint as this will not only avoid unsightly dead stem (with the chance of rot running back down the stem) but will encourage new growth from that joint, again with little chance of rot damaging it.

Experts generally recommend that the cutting should be taken from a non-flowering stem. But while there are several good reasons for this there are equally good reasons for taking cuttings from a stem that has flowered. A non-flowering stem is generally younger and, therefore, more active and vigorous so that it has a good chance of forming roots quickly. Also, if it is not ready to flower the distance between nodes is invariably shorter than it would be once flowers begin to develop, which gives the opportunity to create a more compact plant with early side shoots closer to soil level.

On the other hand, if the stem has not flowered it is not possible to be sure the cutting will flower true to type, or indeed that it will flower at all. Before flowering the stem generally carries only single leaf joints, with a potential side shoot from

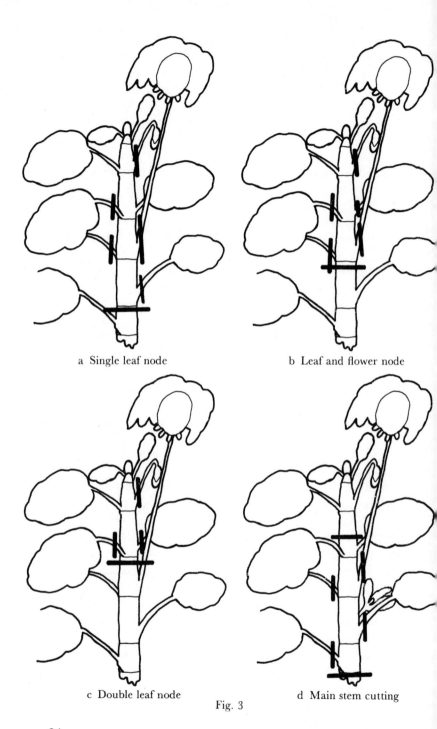

a Single leaf node

b Leaf and flower node

c Double leaf node

d Main stem cutting

Fig. 3

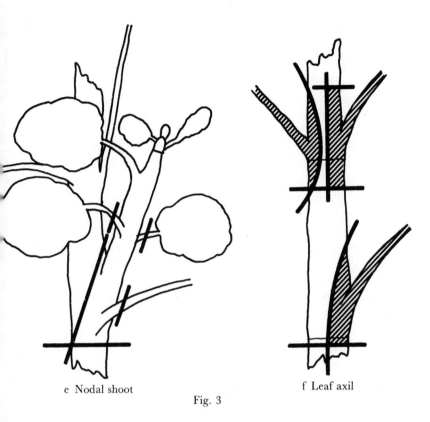

e Nodal shoot

f Leaf axil

Fig. 3

each, but once it has flowered alternate leaf joints will have two leaves, with the potential of a side shoot from each. Two side shoots from a double leaf joint are slightly preferable as they create a more balanced effect, but as leaf joints opposite a flower stem seldom carry a side shoot no extra side shoots are obtained.

If both flowering and non-flowering stems are used for cuttings, it is possible to propagate throughout the year and at the same time prune the flowering plants, preventing them from becoming untidy and misshapen. Other than for regals, which are discussed later, there appears to be no good reason to be dogmatic about where cuttings should come from. They should be taken from the most suitable point of the parent plant, irrespective of whether it is a flowering shoot or not.

Figures 3a–e, pages 24–5, show the principal types of cutting available and while they have been illustrated as flowering stems (apart from 3e), those in 3a, 3b and 3d could equally well be non-flowering stems. The base of a cutting may be trimmed to a single leaf joint (3a), a type of cutting more likely to be found on a non-flowering stem in spring. Once flowering has started, as illustrated, such cuttings are normally too long on zonals, except on dwarf or miniature varieties, where they are often ideal. While a plant is flowering the cutting often has to be trimmed to a leaf and flower joint (3b) to get the ideal length. These, it will be found, root just as easily as any other type of cutting but seldom branch from below soil level, as all the other types of cutting discussed here are likely to do—or at least are potentially capable of doing.

On occasions, some varieties develop with very long distances between leaf joints in which case it may be necessary to restrict the cutting to only three joints, which usually involves trimming at a double leaf joint (3c). This is most often necessary with ivy-leaved varieties and some of the older types of zonals.

The main-stem types of cutting (3d) is most frequently available towards the end of the growing season when the parent plant is being cut back for the winter, but occasionally can be obtained in early or mid season when one stem of a plant grows too strongly in relation to the remainder and has to be removed. On those occasions when the cutting is longer than that illustrated, it is possible that the top section may itself have been used as a cutting, leaving a healthy section of main stem which can form an excellent cutting if trimmed top and bottom.

The nodal shoot cutting (3e) is perhaps the ideal, as it is invariably young, healthy and short-jointed and has a high potential for producing additional basal shoots, so welcome when growing bushy specimen pot plants. It is suitable for all types of geraniums, particularly regals, although some growers do prefer to allow the shoot to grow on a little and take the cuttings at the first double leaf joint.

Trimming of the cutting should always be done with the sharp knife. Firstly, however, it is preferable to remove as many stipules as possible; this is best achieved by placing the blade of the knife between main stem and stipule, then trapping the stipule by pressing it against the blade with your thumb. A slight outward and downward movement of the blade should bring the complete stipule away from the stem without diffi-culty—practice quickly makes perfect.

Cuttings should always be handled with gentle care, as such young fresh growth is very easily bruised and bruising can so quickly lead to rotting of the cutting once potted. Leaves can be removed by being pulled down and away from the stem, but this method requires the cutting to be held firmly in the other hand and the stem is liable to bruising there; and the young stem at the actual leaf joint may also get bruised. So leaves and flower stems should always be trimmed with a sharp knife or blade whenever possible, holding the cutting at the bottom below the level of the intended lowest joint. The blade of the knife should be placed against the stem above the intended cut and drawn gently but firmly downwards, removing the leaf as close to the stem as possible.

It is not necessary to leave more than two or three leaves on any cutting. Remember, a plant transpires through its leaves and as its water intake will be severely restricted until new roots are formed, the available leaf surface is best reduced to a minimum. Any sign of a shoot beginning to form at a leaf joint which will be at or below soil level is best rubbed off with a finger, as otherwise it is likely to rot off and spread to the main stem.

The final cut should be the base of the cutting, after removing all leaves and flowers. This cut should be as close as possible below the leaf joint selected which will be marked by the thin scar left by the removal of the stipule.

The cutting will root satisfactorily in various media, from plain water to sand, perlite, vermiculite, peat or any prepared compost, either soil-based or soilless. Actually, cuttings taken from garden plants will usually root well if a small hole is made within 6 in of the parent plant, a pinch of sand dropped into the base of this hole and the cutting then inserted, firmed-in gently and lightly watered. Once the cutting can be seen to be growing on, usually after about six weeks, it should be lifted with a small ball of soil to a more suitable position. It is more usual, however, for cuttings to be rooted in a greenhouse or similar situation and almost certainly the most satisfactory all-round rooting medium is one of the proprietary soilless composts, such as J. Arthur Bowers, with about 20 per cent additional coarse sand well mixed in. Alternatively, any compost prepared for seeds, such as John Innes seed compost, will be suitable.

Preferably each cutting should be grown in its own pot and 2 in is an ideal size for all geraniums, except perhaps miniatures which will be quite happy in a smaller 'thumb' pot. Other methods such as four or five cuttings around the edge of a 4 inch pot, or a dozen or so in a seed tray, are certainly suitable for rooting cuttings but, unfortunately, the risk of root damage and resulting check in growth when moving the cuttings on to their subsequent pot is unnecessarily high if small individual pots are available as an alternative. The compost should be lightly packed into the pot (one tap on the bench is sufficient to settle it) and then stood in a little water until the surface is obviously wet. Then the pot should be removed and surplus water allowed to drain off in the shade for an hour or so. After this a small hole should be made in the centre of the compost about half an inch deep, sufficient only to hold the cutting firmly in an upright position. Insert the cutting until the base is touching the bottom of the small hole and firm the compost gently towards the stem of the cutting rather than downwards. The pot and cutting should then be placed in full shade for about three days before being given normal light. Within four weeks, often sooner, the cutting will have rooted and can be moved to a larger pot. During this period a fine spray of clear water every other day will be welcomed by the cuttings, except in the winter months when it is not needed and might encourage rot.

The reason for the pinch of sand in the bottom of the hole made for the cutting, or the additional sand in the cutting compost, is that sand appears to aggravate and stimulate the base of the cutting to form roots more quickly. If you experiment by placing a spare cutting in a small glass jar containing about half an inch of plain water, you can observe how the roots form and develop, and will become aware of exactly what is happening to the cuttings in the pots. The water should be replaced every seven days to keep it fresh and if you should wish to grow-on such a cutting it is advisable carefully to move it on into compost in a 2 in or $2\frac{1}{2}$ in pot as soon as the first root is about $\frac{1}{4}$ in long.

Growers do not always agree on whether the trimmed cuttings should be inserted into the compost immediately or left on a shaded bench for twenty-four hours to callous over, as recommended by many older gardeners and gardening writers. Both opinions are probably right—and wrong. A cutting taken from a greenhouse plant, to be rooted in the same or similar environment, does not appear to benefit from lying around the greenhouse for a day before being inserted into the compost. On the other hand, the normally lusher condition of a cutting from a garden plant can cause it to look 'off-colour' for a while if immediately inserted into compost in greenhouse conditions, and such cuttings do seem to benefit from a brief time spent on the bench before potting.

To use or not to use hormone rooting powder is another area of disagreement among growers. Almost certainly it contributes little to the rooting process of geranium cuttings. But as most proprietary rooting powders contain Captan, or a similar ingredient, to protect against rot, to which geranium cuttings are susceptible, their use is probably a useful and welcome precaution.

There is one further method of vegetative propagation not yet mentioned, the use of the leaf axil (Figure 3f, page 25). It is known that most leaf joints have a high meristem activity and are potentially capable of producing a shoot. The principle is to cut away a leaf joint with a section of the stem, trim it neatly and insert it into a tray or single pot with the leaf remaining attached and facing upwards. The shaded areas in the illustration indicate the various alternative ways of removing the 'cutting'. The success rate of leaf-axil propagation is not outstanding and the method is not particularly recommended unless mass-reproduction is both essential and urgent. It can be successful, however, although the resulting plants will take at least six weeks longer to reach maturity. You have, of course, little more than a nodal shoot cutting (Figure 3e) without the shoot, and as such it can produce a bushy plant once established. A leaf axil on which a small side shoot has actually broken through is unlikely to succeed, as rot will almost certainly occur around this new growth.

During the period that the cutting is in the original rooting compost it is preferable to water from the bottom rather than to trickle water on to the compost surface. Small pots dry out quickly and it is advisable to look at them daily. If they are dry, stand them in a tray or bowl containing about $\frac{1}{4}$ in of water until the compost surface is obviously damp and then remove immediately.

Propagators that provide bottom heat are an advantage, but by no means essential for cuttings to be rooted between April and September. If the propagator is fitted with a hood or can otherwise be tightly closed in, it is best to remove the hood entirely or raise it sufficiently to allow good ventilation, as geraniums do not enjoy high humidity. When using a propagator, watering must be done even more carefully, although undersoil heating in a sand or peat bed, which is itself kept damp, is a great help. However, propagators do not necessarily increase the success rate with cuttings, except in late autumn and winter, and once about nine in every ten of your cuttings 'takes', you would be well advised to stick with the method you are using, whether it involves a propagator or not.

This of course prompts the question as to the best time to take cuttings and, as usual with geraniums, the answer is hardly straightforward. Much depends on the availability of cuttings and the purpose for which the resulting plant is required. Bedding zonals usually start their life as cuttings in early September, especially if their parent plant is already being used as a bedder, at which time suitable cuttings will be most abundant. The greatest difficulty for beginners at this time is steeling themselves to cut back a plant which may very well be in full flower and still have a couple of months potential flowering ahead. Those with heated propagators will get away with October cuttings but may regret the missing six weeks when planting out the following May—you can't have your cake and eat it.

If there is a choice of plants of the particular variety from which cuttings are to be taken, then select the parent plant(s) carefully. The importance of stock selection should not be underestimated for all cuttings, irrespective of the type but taking into account the purpose for which the plant will be required. Bedding zonal cuttings required from the current year's bedding plants are easily selected if attention has been paid to the plants during the summer. Almost certainly one or two will have performed better than their companions and these should have been marked with a label or small stake as sources of the best cutting material. Similarly, if you have plants grown in pots, those that performed best should have been marked. If the cutting is to be grown on as a pot plant, however, it may be necessary to avoid individual weaker or stronger stems, even on a selected plant. This particularly applies to the miniature and dwarf types. Tricolour and bicolour types may be selected as cuttings from individual stems of different plants in an effort to obtain the uniformity or brilliance of colour required in future plants.

Similarly, regals should be selected as potential stock plants during their first flowering, taking account both of growing habit and quality of flower, and the better plants should be cut back hard immediately after that first flowering. They may then be stood outside—a bed of ashes in a garden frame or protected situation is ideal—or kept in the greenhouse. After about eight or ten weeks, generally in August, these plants should provide adequate cuttings of the nodal shoot type (Fig. 3e) which can be taken with a portion of the main stem or from the first pair of double leaves.

When to take cuttings of plants required to grow on as pot plants depends very much on when the resulting plant is required to be at its best. Ideally, a full ten to twelve months from cutting to flowering should be allowed, but varieties differ and more detailed information on timing appears on pages 68 to 70. The most suitable short-jointed and vigorous cuttings are invariably available in spring each year, but to take these delays the flowering of the parent plant for ten to fourteen weeks and generally means the cuttings have to be grown-on for over twelve months to obtain a truly specimen plant in flower. During the pre-flowering period of the new plant you will again have been faced with the same problem of whether to take cuttings. In fact, of course, geranium cuttings are plentiful throughout the year and beginners are more likely to acquire a surplus of plants than a shortage. Certainly once a few plants of a variety from selected stock have been built up, one such plant is usually available to provide cuttings whenever required.

The final information required in any chapter on propagation is on when propagation is complete and cultivation begins. Cultivation can start in earnest from the moment the cutting has established an adequate root system. It is sometimes obvious that it is growing-on, as new leaves break and develop on the cutting and it takes on an almost perky appearance. It is more usual actually to check that roots have formed, which necessitates knocking the ball of compost out of the pot. The simplest way to do this is to place the first two fingers across the top of the pot one on either side of the cutting, gently trapping and holding it between them. Turn the pot upside-down and tap the rim of the pot on the edge of a bench. This should free the compost from the pot sides and enable the pot (still upside-down) to be lifted free without disturbing the compost. If roots have reached the outside of the compost the cutting is ready to be moved to a larger pot; if not the original pot should be carefully replaced over the compost, turned the right way up and tapped on the bench to firm the compost. This operation should never be attempted when the compost is dry; the ideal time is about twenty-four hours after the cutting has been watered.

That it is not possible to do this test with a tray of cuttings is another good reason for using an individual pot for each one. Cuttings in a tray are best left for about six weeks or until the majority appear to be growing-on, at which point they can be moved into individual pots. Never tug at any cutting, however gently, to determine if it has secured itself with roots: if it hasn't, you will only succeed in breaking off any small roots just starting or disturbing the cutting sufficiently to set it back, if not lose it altogether.

Finally, always insert a clear label in the pot at the time the cutting is inserted, giving the name of the variety and perhaps, on the reverse, the date the cutting was taken. Unless you enjoy suspense it can be frustrating to wait ten months to find out the variety of a particular plant.

GROWING FROM SEED

Geraniums can be grown from seed as easily as from cuttings although, in the case of bought seed, it was a very hit-and-miss affair until the late 1960s, when F1 hybrids first became generally available by way of the 'Carefree' strain of zonal geraniums.

It is still possible to buy random geranium seed cheaply, but however reputable the source, you cannot be guaranteed satisfaction with the resultant plants. Any amateur hybridist will tell you that even selected breeding from the better varieties produces widely inconsistent results, as regards both flower and plant habit. However, the suspense of a hybridist's life can be yours very cheaply if you have the time and space available; the delights and disappointments as the plants come into flower should be experienced by every geranium grower. Collecting seed from your own existing varieties is more rewarding once you have a collection, but this will be discussed in Chapter 10.

Seeds of F1 hybrids are a different matter. The seedsman *can* guarantee the flower and habit of the plant which the seeds will produce. They are also a different matter as regards price, unfortunately, as you get very few seeds in a relatively expensive packet. But for your outlay, you will obtain reasonably uniform germination and plant habit, with a prior knowledge of the flower colour and type (unless you have bought a packet of mixed colours, of course). Much time and money have been invested in the development and production of the modern F1 hybrids and the improvements during the 1970s have been remarkable. However they have been produced with the commercial grower in mind and this should be remembered when considering the timing, temperatures and methods of cultivation recommended. Up to 1980 only zonal geraniums were available as F1 hybrids and only single-flowered varieties at that. This is not unnatural, given the annual volume of bedding geraniums required, although the smaller market for pot plants is also well served by these F1s.

Whatever the source of your seeds, whether F1 hybrids, more traditional random seed packets or seeds collected from your own plants, the methods of growing can be the same. The date on which seeds are sown does vary, however, depending on the growing conditions and the date on which the flowering plant is required. Generally, commercial growers will aim to have most of their plants available, with the first flower just showing, for mid-May. To achieve this, germination temperatures of 70° to 75°F (21° to 24°C) are required and growing-on temperatures of 64° to 70°F (18° to 21°C). The 64°F is the minimum acceptable night temperature. With such conditions and a couple of applications of a rather expensive dwarfing agent (Cycocel is normally used), the mid-May flowering can be achieved from an early January sowing.

If you have, or are willing to maintain, that level of winter temperature, then the five-month programme used by commercial growers would be equally suitable for you. A couple of dozen geranium seeds would not on their own justify the expenditure involved, however, and most home growers, with an approximate winter greenhouse temperature of 40°F (4°C) and perhaps no bottom heat for germination, would find that a growing period similar to that required for cuttings would be more suitable, equally effective and much less costly!

Indeed, the commonest (and unjustified) claim against bought seed is that the plants flower too late in the year, and this is almost certainly because the seeds have been purchased, along with next year's annuals and vegetables, around Christmas or later, with little hope of providing adequate temperatures to produce the plants for June. Most amateurs will find that a late July to early August sowing of seeds should safely produce F1 hybrids for bedding or pot plants from early June onwards without difficulty; in fact the plants will be better for their more leisurely progress. Other types of geranium seed sown at the same time will similarly be coming into flower from that date onwards, but as you will have little idea what to expect from these it is unwise to bank on the plants meeting any particular need, such as bedding.

The seeds are large enough to plant individually, $\frac{1}{2}$ to 1 in apart, in a seed tray, about $\frac{1}{4}$ in deep, in any suitably well-drained seed compost. Covering the tray with a sheet of glass maintains the humidity and prevents the compost drying out too rapidly. The seedlings may 'damp-off' if this high humidity is maintained once they have emerged, so it is advisable every other day to prick out seedlings whose cotyledon leaves have opened. The seedlings will emerge from a few days to a few weeks after sowing and it is well worth persevering with the tray of seeds for as long as ten weeks, watering as necessary and replacing the glass. It is then necessary to take particular care when pricking out seedlings to remove as little compost as possible so as not to disturb other seeds. The seedlings can be potted directly into individual 2 in or $2\frac{1}{2}$ in pots and from then on treated exactly as you would treat a cutting, potting-on after about six weeks.

'Springtime', an 'Irene'-type zonal, very popular in Britain as a bedder and pot plant *(Pat Brindley)*

Two flower heads of the double-flowered zonal, 'Harvester', an old, pale salmon-pink, bedding variety, with large well shaped blooms *(H. Smith)*

'Joy', one of William Schmidt's earlier regal introductions (1955). A bright, salmon-orange flower with a pronounced white throat; the picture shows clearly the frilled or wavy petal edge that can add so much to the beauty of regal flowers *(Pat Brindley)*

3 Composts, Pots and Potting-on

Geraniums are tolerant plants and, treated properly, will perform adequately for six months or more in a pot of standard potting compost. But they prefer the compost to be slightly acid—a pH of 6.7 is ideal (pH 7 is neutral). Most commercial composts available are within an acceptable range, if perhaps a little low on lime, but avoid composts prepared specifically for cacti and other lime-loving plants. It is better not to try to adjust the lime content (pH) of the compost if you are inexperienced; if it is known to be lime-deficient, add a half-teaspoonful of garden lime to each gallon of water at every watering, remembering to stir well.

Most garden soils are suitable for geraniums, too, but one of the simple soil-analysis kits available will confirm the position. If the pH is low, lime can be added, and if it is too high a dressing of sulphate of ammonia or liberal addition of peat should correct the position.

The choice of composts available in which geraniums can be grown might appear wide but is not really so. They are either soilless, consisting almost entirely of peat, or soil-based, such as the John Innes composts, the main constituent of which is loam. The John Innes composts merit brief mention, although anyone particularly interested in composts will find several interesting and informative books on the market. Basically, the JI composts are formulations for making up four grades of loam-based composts suitable for most pot-grown subjects. The four grades are potting composts numbers 1, 2 and 3 and a seed compost. The first three consist of the basic bulk items measured by volume: 7 parts of loam, 3 parts of peat and 2 parts of sand, to which is added one, two or three standard measures of JI base fertilizer and chalk per bushel (8 gallons) respectively.

The base fertilizer can usually be purchased ready-mixed,

but consists of the following ingredients, measured by weight: 2 parts coarse hoof and horn grist, 2 parts superphosphate of lime and 1 part sulphate of potash. A standard measure consists of 4 ounces of this mixture with $\frac{3}{4}$ ounce of chalk which should be added to each bushel of the bulk items and left for a week before use.

John Innes Compost No 1 is suitable for initial potting after rooting, but subsequent and final potting is preferable in John Innes No 2, although No 1 or No 3 would suffice. The John Innes Seed Compost, which is suitable for rooting geranium cuttings, is made up of 2 parts by volume of loam, 1 part of peat and 1 part of sand, to which is added $1\frac{1}{2}$ ounces of superphosphate of lime and $\frac{3}{4}$ ounce of chalk. All the loam, peat and sand used in JI composts should have been sterilized and, of course, the quality of these ingredients is of the utmost importance. The reliability of the source ultimately becomes your only guarantee of quality, whether you purchase the basic ingredients for making up yourself or buy ready-mixed compost for immediate use.

It was probably the natural variations in the loam available for such composts that brought about the introduction of the far more consistent soilless composts. The University of California is often given much of the credit for the development of these; some years ago they were often described as UC composts. They have many advantages for commercial growers and it is almost certainly this aspect that has created the current popularity.

Soilless composts, now obtainable from every garden shop or centre, are perfectly suitable for growing geraniums in pots, given a little more care in watering and feeding. Basically, these composts consist of fine peat, sometimes with sand added, and a base fertilizer similar to that used in the JI composts, but with added trace elements to replace those absent or deficient due to the omission of loam. As sand has a higher weight-to-volume ratio than peat, it has been reduced or omitted entirely in many proprietary soilless composts, and the addition of one part in ten by volume of horticultural (not builders') sand before potting geraniums would certainly not go amiss.

The relative advantages and disadvantages of these two types of compost are reasonably obvious. Soilless composts, while easier and more pleasant to handle and more consistent in performance, nevertheless require more attention to feeding as the nutrients are washed out quite rapidly by watering. They are also more suitable for capillary watering. Soil-based composts generally require the pots to be crocked and are heavier to handle. Feeding, however, is much less critical, and after the plants have been potted the weight of course becomes an advantage, holding them more securely—particularly once they are full grown. Geraniums often become top-heavy when grown in soilless compost. Undoubtedly soilless compost encourages faster and lusher growth, which is a definite advantage in the earlier months of a geranium's life, but as it matures it would benefit from a slower, woodier growth, particularly for the flowers—they last longer when 'harder'. There is therefore a case for changing to soil-based compost for final potting, but this is not always successful and can give a set-back to the plant.

POTS—CLAY OR PLASTIC?

Pots are also available in 'ancient and modern' versions. The clay pot has become increasingly scarce and difficult to buy, is more expensive and certainly heavier and less convenient to handle than the modern plastic equivalent. However, the stability provided by a clay pot is a distinct advantage, as is its porous nature which, besides assisting ventilation, also keeps roots cooler in hot weather. The porosity does mean that clay pots become unsightly with salt deposits and algae and are a problem to clean even when empty, more so when they have a plant in them. They also require more frequent watering, although the dangers of overwatering are considerably reduced and the old gardening habit of tapping a clay pot for a clear 'ring', which indicates that watering is required, helps to remove a lot of doubt.

To summarize, if it is accepted that air, or more correctly the oxygen in the air, is one of the most important constituents of a plant's requirements (for the nourishment of the roots and the release of plant foods in the compost), then clay pots and soil-based composts appear to create better environments for a plant to live in. Almost all the advantages associated with soilless composts and plastic pots appear to be for the benefit of the grower and all the advantages of good soil-based composts and clay pots for the benefit of the plant. So—it is hardly surprising that most readers (and authors) will continue to try and master the greater intricacies associated with soilless composts and plastic pots, trusting that the geranium really is as tolerant as this author insists it is.

POTTING-ON

Having decided on the type of compost and pot to use, you can return to that cutting that had developed a rooting system and was ready for moving into a larger pot ('potting-on').

The only decision still to be made is the size of the next pot. It is often suggested that plants should be moved on gradually to their final pot. This compels the roots to make maximum use of the available compost at each stage of growth, saves greenhouse space and appears to prevent the plant becoming too lush and vigorous in growth, so the suggestion is soundly based and worth following. However, the size of the final pot in which you intend to allow the plant to flower will have a bearing on the sizes you choose for the intermediate pot or pots, as it is awkward and messy if the new pot is not at least 1 in larger than its predecessor.

The following recommendations on progressive pot sizes should prove helpful.

Miniature varieties are generally restricted to a $3\frac{1}{2}$ in final pot, as most of them look too small for the pot in anything larger. Indeed show schedules normally specify that miniatures must not be exhibited in a pot exceeding $3\frac{1}{2}$ in. Having rooted the cutting in a thumb pot ($1\frac{1}{2}$ in diameter), there is really only one intermediate size available, $2\frac{1}{2}$ in. The miniature plants therefore progress from $1\frac{1}{2}$ in, to $2\frac{1}{2}$ in to $3\frac{1}{2}$ in pots.

Dwarf varieties are normally taken up to $4\frac{1}{2}$ in pots for flowering and, again, exhibitors are restricted to this size. The cuttings go into a 2 in pot, then move to a 3 in intermediate pot and finally into the $4\frac{1}{2}$ in pot.

Basic varieties are usually flowered in 5 in or 6 in pots, the more vigorous varieties requiring the larger size to do themselves justice. If you intend restricting the plant to a 5 in pot, the suggested progression is 2 in to $3\frac{1}{2}$ in to 5 in, but ideally plants of this type are more suited to the larger final pot and after the $3\frac{1}{2}$ in should be moved to a $4\frac{1}{2}$ in and then to the 6 in. This type can be grown to advantage in even larger pots; a final pot of 7 in would follow on from the 5 in, or an 8 in final pot from the 6 in.

Ivy-leaved varieties follow the normal potting progression except that they appear to prefer half pots or dwarf (three-quarter height) pots once the cutting has rooted. It is very difficult to obtain 3 in dwarf pots, however, so that the intermediate pot for dwarf ivy-leaved varieties should be a dwarf $3\frac{1}{2}$ in pot when available.

Plants intended for bedding out can usually be kept in the pre-final pot size if the cutting is not taken until the autumn. However, the miniatures and dwarf varieties will be happier if they can be given an extra $\frac{1}{2}$ in—miniature in 3 in and dwarf in 4 in. Before planting out it is preferable to harden the plants in a garden frame for a fortnight, giving them a good watering the day before you intend moving them to their final situation.

Actually a strong case can be made for all dwarf and basic types to be put into dwarf pots between cutting pot and final pot, when a real 'specimen' plant is required. The principal reason for this is that at the intermediate stage or stages the restricted pot depth forces the roots to make better use of the available compost and makes even more fresh compost available to them when the plant is moved into its final pot. A plant does spend much longer in its final pot than any other and has far more top growth, as well as flowers, to sustain during that period, so the more compost available to the roots the better. If the plants are ultimately intended for setting up in a hanging basket, it is virtually essential that the intermediate pots are half or dwarf pots, due to the restricting depth of most baskets. The basket itself should be regarded as the final pot and while it is possible to achieve an excellent basket from a single, centrally planted, ivy-leaved variety, it is simpler and more usual to use four smaller plants, three evenly spaced around the edge of the basket and the other planted centrally. The compost for hanging baskets need be no different from that selected for final potting, especially if the modern, one-piece, plastic basket is used. Many of these have the advantage of an integral water tray which also enables them to stand easily on a greenhouse staging while the plant is being shaped and trained; there is no need to hang them until the trailing shoots have reached the bench. The mesh baskets lined with green or black polythene are similar, but if sphagnum moss is available it should always be used. When used with John Innes compost a thin layer of saturated peat ($\frac{1}{4}$ in is sufficient) is beneficial between the moss and the compost, and perhaps even an additional one part in 10 extra peat added, as these baskets do dry out quickly and the extra peat helps.

An important part of this chapter must be to discuss how long the plant should, or could, remain in each pot. There is one non-variable point: as soon as the original cutting's roots reach the base of its first pot, and before they start circling around the inside of the pot, it should be moved to a larger one. This will probably be no more than six weeks from the date the cutting was inserted, less if bottom heat has been used throughout rooting.

Ideally, that is the right and proper time to move to each successive size pot, but as the date on which the plant is required to flower is often of importance, other factors have to be considered—there is little point in having bedders in full bloom a couple of months before they can be planted out. Most geraniums should have just reached their peak after six months in their final pot, perhaps five months in the case of a dwarf or miniature. A plant tends not to flower before it has filled its pot with roots, so that once in its final pot it will generally continue to develop until the roots reach the sides and bottom, and then begin to think about producing flowers. It could be up to three more months before most stems are carrying full flowerheads.

A cutting taken on 1 June one year and intended as a pot plant to flower during the next summer will, therefore, require twelve months from cutting to full bloom. Of this period, the plant will have spent about one month in the cutting pot and six months in the final pot, leaving five months in intermediate stage(s). While a miniature or dwarf geranium might tolerate five months in only one intermediate pot, it is really too long, and certainly so for a basic type. If basic-type plants are to be kept growing steadily from cutting to flowering, two to three months in an intermediate pot is quite sufficient. So that in the example being considered, there is little choice but to use two intermediate pots for basic types, which virtually demands the plant must finish in a 6 in pot.

The necessity for some forethought is now apparent. Before taking a cutting the 'when and where' of the final plant should be considered. A plant required to brighten the windowsill of your home during the summer will probably be a miniature, a dwarf or a basic type that is suited to a 5 in pot. Almost all varieties within that category require only a ten-month growing period to reach full flower, three months only having been spent in just one intermediate pot stage. If you are lucky enough to have a home with wide windowsills or other suitable indoor situations that will accommodate a 6 in pot, then of course the 1 June cutting would have been ideal. Otherwise a 1 August cutting would work out better.

Similar thought will be required by anyone hoping for a plant to display at the local or some other show, but more detailed information on timing geraniums for shows is given in Chapter 8.

Plants intended for bedding out are subject to different considerations if, as suggested, the pot has been kept down to intermediate size. This, of course, is a winter space-saving suggestion: if you have ample heated winter and spring space available, bedding plants would obviously benefit by being grown to first-flower stage in their normal final pot. This would require the cuttings to be taken earlier than is customary, however, to obtain the ten-month growing period. Most often, bedding plants have no more than eight months in a pot, if cuttings are not taken until mid-September for planting out mid-May. The intermediate pot (3 in for a miniature, 4 in for a dwarf and $4\frac{1}{2}$ in for a basic) becomes virtually the final one, as the plant should be just beginning to flower at the time it is planted out. As the smaller pot is not required to support the plant in flower, a longer spell in it than is normally recommended will not matter.

All the above timings assume that the plant will have been grown on through the winter period with night temperatures between 35°F (2°C) and 45°F (7°C). During this period and at these temperatures growth will be minimal. If higher temperatures can be maintained (and afforded!) more growth will occur, proportionate to the increase in temperature, which could have the effect of shortening the previous suggested growing period by up to a month.

While it is not usual to attempt to flower geraniums during the winter, a few zonal varieties do perform reasonably well if grown specifically for that purpose, although they are unlikely to satisfy you if maximum light is not available and the minimum temperature is allowed to drop below 55°F (13°C). Equally, as they do not have the winter period to contend with during their normal development, they can quite easily be brought to Christmas flowering from cuttings taken in April or May.

Having decided the next pot size and the approximate date for moving into it, the actual process of potting-on is simplicity itself. Firstly, however, check that the roots of the plant really have developed sufficiently to justify the larger pot. As in the case of cuttings, place a hand over the top of the pot with the main stem between the fingers, turn the plant upside down and tap the edge of the pot lightly on the edge of the bench. It should then be possible to lift the pot away from the plant, leaving the roots clearly visible. If they have not reached the bottom, replace the pot and allow the plant to grow on for two or three weeks before examining again.

It is more likely that the plant will be ready for a larger pot. This should be three-quarters filled with loose compost and a suitably sized hole made with the hands by *gently* lifting and firming the compost against the sides of the pot so that it is raised to rim level. It is worth checking that the hole is wide and deep enough to receive the plant by dropping the empty pot into the hole made. The top of the two pots should be level without undue pressure being applied. Then the pot can be tapped lightly on the bench, with the first pot still in the hole, to firm the compost slightly. Lift out the empty pot and, supporting the ball of compost as much as possible, lower the plant into the hole: it should fit neatly, with just a little space to spare. Two firm taps on the bench should cause the compost to fall into that space and the job is done, unless a little extra compost is required to top up to the required level.

One tip that you should never need to use if you have planned ahead properly, but which nevertheless seems to come into use more than once a year for one reason or another, concerns moving the plant from its pot into one only half an inch larger. Firstly, knock the plant out of its pot, then place a little compost at the bottom of the larger pot so that the rims are level when the original pot is stood inside on this compost. Leaving one pot inside the other, stand the pots on the bulk compost and begin to trickle compost into the space between the two pots, occasionally tapping them on a bench to settle and firm the compost. Continue until the compost has reached the rim, tap again and then lift out the smaller pot. You can easily check that no spaces have been left (if they have replace the pot and add more

44

compost) before gently lowering in the plant with its original ball of compost, and finally tapping the pot again to merge the old and new composts. A fiddling job certainly, but no more so than any other method, and it both ensures that no air pockets occur and causes minimal root disturbance.

Finally, both the new compost and that already in the pot should have been well watered beforehand, but not made so wet that water can be squeezed out. If the plant has been watered about 24 hours before potting-on this should be ideal, and the new pot need not be watered for a couple of days. After that it can be well watered to settle the compost further.

4 Cultivation— Ten Golden Rules

Left to its own devices any geranium plant, grown on as advised so far, will reach maturity and flower, but the shape each variety adopts depends on its own inbuilt characteristics. Unfortunately, apart from a few dwarf and regal varieties and even fewer of other types, most geraniums will by nature grow as a single stem until flowering, and will develop into a rather disappointing plant.

TEN GOLDEN RULES
The plants must therefore be persuaded to develop in a more desirable way, and the following ten rules should provide a sound basis by which to produce worthwhile plants. The initial letters of the rules spell 'craftiness', but there is nothing crafty about them; they are purely basic principles and should be developed as good habits that are followed automatically. They are given in no specific order of importance, each being equally valuable in the growing of an acceptable plant during the time that it spends in a pot, whether in a greenhouse or conservatory or on a windowsill.

Clear *enough space*
Every plant should be given its own territory so that it is not touching or growing into its neighbour. If too near the next plant it will be forced to grow very upright, whereas it should be encouraged to spread itself, particularly in its early life. There is no point in trying to excuse a poorly grown plant by saying that you don't have enough space—the space available is fixed, but the number of plants you choose to grow is flexible. So throw out all those tomatoes, fuschias, carnations, begonias and gloxinias and give important plants like geraniums a chance! It may even be necessary to discard the weaker ger-

anium plants to create enough space between the better plants as they develop rapidly in the spring.

Remove *dying leaves and flowers*
Leaves, flowers and stipules have a limited life, and while good cultivation can prolong that life, they will sooner—in the case of flowers—or later—for leaves and stipules—begin to die off. They should then be removed, as not only do they look unsightly but if left on the plant they may begin to decay and cause rot to spread into the main stem or surrounding flowers and foliage.

Adequate *ventilation is vital*
The fact that geraniums are not hardy often encourages the assumption that they must be pampered. This is not so and they positively respond to a free and continual movement of air which helps the leaves to transpire and prevents high humidity, a condition geraniums can well do without. This rule could equally well have been phrased as 'Avoid draughts', and exactly when ventilation becomes a draught must be considered.

A draught in this context is a direct flow of cold air around a plant. The plant can be immediately in front of an open side vent and probably not be in a draught if more than one other vent is open, as this will break up the flow of air. Roof vents do not generally create harmful draughts as they are above plant height, but doors and side vents can cause draughts and are, therefore, best opened as widely as possible and all together when conditions are suitable. When outside conditions are not suitable, a small fan left running in a greenhouse is beneficial.

Feed *frequently*
All geraniums in pots should be fed (or fertilized if you prefer) frequently; at every watering is the most convenient method and has much to recommend it. Actually plants should not require feeding for the first five or six weeks in a new pot as most composts have sufficient quick-release nutrients available for this period. But thereafter regular feeding is essential in soilless composts and strongly recommended in John Innes.

During the time you are building up a plant before flowering, use a high-nitrogen fertilizer with the phosphate and potash balanced. A suitable proportion of available nitrogen, phosphate and potash (NPK) would be 2 (or $1\frac{1}{2}$): 1:1 and several

47

proprietary soluble powders or liquid fertilizers of this formulation are available. The quantity recommended by the manufacturers should be followed but divided by the number of times each plant is being watered, on average, during the recommended feeding period. In the summer you may find you are watering most plants two (or three) times a week, so that if the fertilizer application recommended is one teaspoon to a gallon of water once a week, use a half (or third) of a teaspoon to each gallon for each watering.

About two months before you expect the plant to flower, the high-nitrogen fertilizer should be replaced by a high-potash formulation (NPK of 1:1:2 is suitable) and this should be maintained evey watering throughout the flowering period.

For tricolour and bicolour zonals, a completely balanced fertilizer (NPK of 1:1:1) throughout the life of the plant is probably more suitable than the changeover method, but this can be inconvenient if only a few such plants are grown; a general feeding programme suitable for the other plants being grown will certainly produce satisfactory results.

Turn *regularly*

All plants grow towards the light, so that in a greenhouse they will turn leaves and flowers south, but in the home directly towards the window. If left undisturbed they will continue doing so until they are so lopsided they are in perpetual danger of falling over. To overcome this, turn the plant at regular intervals. A quarter-turn once a week is a good habit to get into, although turning can usually be reduced to once a fortnight in the winter months when the days are shorter. Plants on windowsills usually have to be turned more frequently as the inward side of the plant receives virtually no direct light and the drawing effect of the light from the window is therefore exaggerated. If you ensure that the plant labels in all the pots always face the same way you can be sure none has been missed, and know where to continue if you are interrupted during this weekly job.

Insecticides

Prevention is always better than cure and so you should apply a systemic insecticide spray or add a systemic insecticide when watering once every three months. Greenfly and whitefly are the principal offenders and Murphy's Systemic can keep these pests at bay.

Never *overwater*

While keeping a growing plant short of water is hardly to be recommended, it is nevertheless, with geraniums, infinitely preferable to overwatering. Geraniums seldom fail to recover from even an extended period without water, although they are unlikely ever to be restored to their former glory. On the other hand, overwatering kills! Indeed, once the compost in a pot is waterlogged it becomes permanently difficult to water correctly again, probably because all the air has been expelled and is never adequately replaced. There are three things which, if done quickly, may save a plant that has been overwatered.

The first is suitable only in mild cases of overwatering but is certainly worth trying. Knock the plant out of its pot and stand it on a folded newspaper, changing the newspaper every 24 hours and keeping the compost in heavy shade. Continue until the compost has obviously completely dried out and then replace it in its pot and do not water again for at least a couple of days. The plant will be set back by this shock treatment but it will normally survive, even if many of its leaves don't.

The second method is to knock the plant out of its pot and allow it to dry out on newspapers for a couple of days, as suggested above. Then knock off the ball of compost (unfortunately many of the roots will go too) until most has been removed. The plant can then be put into a smaller pot in which it might begin to recover, although most of the leaves will have to be removed over the next couple of weeks as they give up the struggle for survival.

The third, and by far the most successful, method is immediately to bed the plant out in the driest area of the garden you can find. But don't water it in please! If that position is unsuitable or inconvenient as a permanent home, it is usually safe to lift and plant elsewhere in the garden after about three weeks.

Examine *regularly*

Just how regularly you can examine each and every plant you are growing depends on how much time you have and how many plants you grow. It is a job that should be done as frequently as possible and, of course, the more often it is done the less time it will take, as fewer tasks will be found outstanding. The purpose of the examination is simply to ensure that all is well with the plant. The more important things to look for are the first signs of pests, from aphids to caterpillar eggs, usually found on the underside of leaves. Early signs of disease are dying or rotting vegetation, on the plant or on the surface of the compost, which has not been obvious from a more superficial inspection and may have caused, or be likely to cause, damage to stems or other leaves. Stems, leaves and flowers that require specific attention, because their growth is being restricted by another stem or for some other reason, are also cases for treatment.

The particular action you take on discovering trouble will be discussed in more detail in subsequent chapters, but whatever is necessary should be done immediately, as that is the purpose of the examination.

Shade (*and light*)

Light is essential to the wellbeing of a geranium plant, not least because the chemical reaction (photosynthesis) it creates is basic to its needs, as with any green plant. However, as with much else in life, you can have too much of a good thing and geraniums grown in a greenhouse or on a south-facing windowsill will benefit from some protection from the sun's rays during the summer (May to mid-September in the UK). Firstly, this prevents excessively high greenhouse temperatures which, despite the malicious rumours the British spread about their own weather, can often rise above 100°F (38°C) in a greenhouse, even with maximum ventilation and shading. Secondly, it protects the flowers. Many of the red-coloured varieties in particular can be quickly discoloured under glass in full sunlight, and they will certainly last longer if given some protection.

Many forms of shading are available, from automatic (light-sensitive) internal roller blinds to the partly used tin of white emulsion left over when the kitchen ceiling was painted. All will serve the purpose to some extent, but in Britain the most widely used type of shading is probably one of the proprietary products produced specifically for the purpose, usually white but sometimes green, many of which can be wiped off with a duster when dry. At least one remarkable product gives a heavy white shading when dry but becomes clear when wet. Hand-operated (as opposed to automatic) internal or external 'blinds' can of course be raised or lowered as the weather requires, but this assumes permanent standby manning, which is often impossible; and anyway it can be forgotten.

Stop *the plants*

'Stopping' plants, removing the growing tip of the stem to stop its headlong rush upwards, will—hopefully—cause the stem to produce two or more side shoots. It will be considered in detail in the next chapter, and is of the utmost importance in growing a well-shaped plant, particularly in the early months of its life.

There you have your 'ten golden rules'. Once adopted as basic routines, they will enable you to increase your satisfaction in growing geraniums several times over.

WATERING

Watering pot plants can be tricky; geraniums are a little better and no worse than most other plants.

How?

If you have been convinced that underwatering is preferable to overwatering (perhaps even if you remain unconvinced) the following method may prove of interest.

The plant pots are permanently stood in reasonably deep containers. Plant-pot saucers are too shallow, but the large and small margarine tubs are excellent for most pot sizes up to $4\frac{1}{2}$ in; 5 in pots and upwards will require a little more ingenuity, but plastic containers that can be adapted abound today—the standard one-gallon plastic 'bottle' suits 5 to 7 in pots admirably if the top is cut off to leave a 3 to 4 in 'bowl', butchers' liver trays are about the same depth, and bulk ice-cream containers can be cut down if too tall. (Discretion normally dictates that Tupperware and similar containers in frequent household use are left where they belong.)

Having obtained sufficient containers you commence 'bottom' watering. The water (a little more than you consider the plant might need) is poured into the containers and the plant is left standing for anything from 20 minutes for $3\frac{1}{2}$ in pots to an hour for 6 in pots, after which time any surplus water should be discarded, or saved for future use if it contains fertilizer (as it should). Capillary action within the compost should have drawn up sufficient liquid to satisfy the plant. Even if the top surface of the compost remains dry do not leave the pots longer than suggested; larger pots, particularly, continue the capillary action even after the principal source of water has been removed, and the surface compost may not appear damp until the following day, if then. If the compost surface is obviously damp and surplus water remains, it is advisable either to turn the container over and stand the pot back on top of it or put the pot alongside the container, both of which should allow surplus water to drain out of the pot rather than back into the container. Geraniums do not appear to like standing in water for long periods.

The advantages of bottom watering are many. Firstly, if your bench is slatted, for greater air circulation, the water that may run through the pot doesn't drip on any plants or other items you may be storing below. The plant which you suspect doesn't need water but are not sure about will take up only what its compost can hold. The leaching effect of the more usual top-watering (pouring the water on to the surface of the compost) is considerably reduced, so preserving nutrients and other elements contained within the compost which might otherwise be washed out. Finally, there is less chance of damaging the leaves, as can happen when you insert the watering-can over the pot rim, and of splashing leaves, which can cause unsightly marks or even burns when the sun falls on the water droplets.

Disadvantages are not as numerous, but the obvious one is that it takes longer to water this way. If the opposite effect to leaching is experienced, salts from the compost being carried upwards and forming a crust on the surface of the compost, it can easily be cured by watering from the top occasionally or as necessary—once a month is generally sufficient to prevent the crust appearing.

Other useful methods are individual trickle watering and capillary matting, both of which can be real time-savers. Unfortunately trickle watering can so easily lead to overwatering and like capillary matting is not really suitable between autumn and late spring, the period when geraniums prefer a very dry atmosphere. Capillary matting can be effective from late spring

First-pip 'Regina' (*Frank Hawley*)

throughout the summer, although it is advisable not to use the reservoir-tank system which keeps the matting permanently wet. The matting is best soaked from a hose and allowed to dry out completely, then soaked again once the pots standing on it have drawn up the water and dried out. Another useful piece of advice to those using capillary matting is to section off the matting, keeping each section for similar-size pots and plants so that they all require about the same amount of water at the same time. Most capillary matting on its own appears insufficient to maintain 5 in or larger pots without additional top watering during the summer.

When?
'Only water geraniums when they need it' is hardly useful advice unless accompanied by some guidance on how to ascertain when they need it. An obvious method is to use one of the excellent small watering indicators, but if many plants are grown this can take a long time as it is really a two-handed operation, necessitating putting down the water-can between each pot. The indicators should therefore be used only with those pots where some doubt exists. These can usually be kept to a minimum by making one or both of the following tests:

If the surface of the compost appears dry, press a finger into it. A damp compost beneath the surface will feel colder to the touch and can therefore be left without watering for another day or so.

The other method will work really well only when you are using the same compost for all plants; if you are, it can prove invaluable. Lift each pot in one hand just before you apply the intended water, and you will quickly learn to assess if the compost is dry from the weight. A damp compost is noticeably heavier than a dry one. While the difference is far more pronounced with soilless compost, it is nevertheless quite apparent with soil-based composts. When this weight method is used it will help if all the pots of a similar size are kept together, as a $3\frac{1}{2}$ in pot among a batch of larger ones will always feel lighter, which may result in overwatering.

It is preferable to water plants in the early evening, or failing

(*above*) 'Aztec', a regal of superb growing habit (*Frank Hawley*). (*below*) A flowerhead of 'Kathleen Gamble', showing the almost-perfect round floret, with shading and veining (*J. Keay*)

that early morning, to give the plant as much time as possible to take up the water before the higher temperatures arrive. However, if a plant is flagging around midday it is essential to water immediately and not wait until 5 pm just because 'early evening is the best time to water'.

This whole book could be filled with the tips that have appeared in the gardening press for watering plants while you are away from home on an extended holiday. Most of them start by recommending that the plants are given 'a good soaking' before your departure which is unfortunate if you grow geraniums—we have already repeatedly warned against overwatering. Plants should certainly be watered immediately before departure and perhaps just this once in the year it is permissible to 'half water' a plant that you are not sure about—the bottom-watering method can be invaluable on such occasions. But resist the temptation to leave plants standing longer, and certainly don't leave them 'paddling' while you go off to do likewise at the seaside.

Certainly, the best method of looking after plants while you are away is to arrange with a fellow geranium enthusiast or other experienced greenhouse plantsman to come along to water them. The only disadvantage of this method is that you will almost certainly be required to repay the compliment, but at least that will remind you what an inconvenience it can be and therefore how lucky you are to have such a friend. Another satisfactory method in most circumstances during the summer is to water the plants as usual immediately before departure, having sunk them to about half their depth in a well-watered flower-bed or child's sandpit. The plants will normally be quite happy outside while you are away, although flowers may be marked or damaged by wind or rain and any exhibitor who wishes to show the plants shortly after his return is best advised to find that friend to water for him—or cancel his holiday!

With what?
As previously mentioned, it is safer to give geraniums a less-than-full-strength fertilizer at each watering. It is unwise to collect rainwater for pot plants as this can contain various impurities or even diseases from the roof area where the rain is collected as well as while it stands outside.

Unless your local domestic water is very hard (having a high lime content) it should be quite suitable if left standing in a tub or other bulk container in the greenhouse for a few hours before being applied. This standing time is to allow the water to reach the ambient greenhouse temperature—tap water direct from the mains can be very cold and give the plants quite a shock. If it should prove necessary to leave a bulk water supply in the greenhouse (or outside) for any length of time, put a little permanganate of potash in the container to avoid algae developing.

SPRAYING

In the spring, as days begin to lengthen and geraniums begin to develop more rapidly, the increasing temperatures should allow you to give the plants an occasional light spray with clear water. It helps to clean and freshen the older leaves, and the plants do seem to respond to this treatment. As you become surer of the warmer weather such spraying can be increased in frequency to once a week, carried out on a warm evening. When flower buds begin to develop spraying is best discontinued. After spraying has started, one of the earliest should contain one teaspoon of Epsom salts (magnesium sulphate) in a gallon of water and this could well be repeated immediately before the buds appear. The foliage will become a noticeably darker green shortly after these applications, which should be heavier than the normal light spray but stop short of wetting to 'run off'. Tricolour zonals are best left out of the Epsom-salt spray so as not to disturb their natural leaf colouring. Similarly, during this period a couple of similar sprays with a Maxicrop dilution, as directed by manufacturers, serve as a good tonic for geraniums. Should either the Epsom salts or Maxicrop leave slight deposits or marks, these are easily washed off if the following week's spray of clear water is applied to any affected leaves a little more powerfully then usual.

FEEDING

Fertilizers should always be applied at the rate recommended by the manufacturers, subject to the previously mentioned adjustment to spread the recommended period over every watering. If you give some fertilizer at every watering you avoid the situation where particular plants are damp enough not to require watering when their 'weekly' feed is due. If that happens, you either water the plant, 'because it won't get any feed for a week otherwise', with the resultant danger of overwatering or, alternatively, have to devise a rather complicated system of remembering which plants require feeding at their next watering.

Apart from the high-nitrogen and high-potash fertilizers discussed in the Ten Golden Rules, other fertilizers can prove quite suitable. Indeed the Epsom salts and Maxicrop sprays can be added to the normal fertilizer and watered into the pot instead of spraying, if preferred. Osmocote, or one of the newer similar products, is an excellent additional reserve or back-up feed which is either mixed into compost or raked into the top of the compost surface (the latter is not really suitable for bottom-watering techniques). The slow release of nutrients over a long period that Osmocote provides is ideally suited to geranium culture, particularly to the miniature and dwarf varieties whose smaller pots naturally restrict the available quantity of initial base fertilizer. If top watering is preferred, it is worth withholding the Osmocote until the plant has been in its final pot for about eight weeks, so lengthening its effectiveness by the same period. This method requires only that the recommended dosage is scattered over the surface of the compost and lightly raked in.

John Innes base fertilizer was formulated many years ago for loam-based composts and, not unnaturally, there have been suppliers who have claimed to improve the original formulae in various ways, especially in recent years since controlled slow-release nutrients have become available. It has not been an easy job to convince gardeners, who have long relied on the consistency which the name John Innes gave to these composts. However, it must be accepted that, within the basic concepts of the John Innes formulae—as valid today as they were initially—technical advances have enabled horticultural suppliers to offer alternative base fertilizers. To many gardeners such a suggestion may border on heresy, but alleged improvements must not be condemned out of hand if we are to obtain the full benefits of the times in which we live.

Peat-based composts with their inherent absence of trace elements have given the innovators a chance, as the JI base on its own is not suitable for them. Those gardeners who make up their own composts, either loam or peat based, should not be afraid to experiment *a little* with new products from reputable sources. They are most unlikely to cause serious harm and far more likely to live up to the manufacturers' claims (after making reasonable allowance for the normal inbuilt enthusiasm associated with advertising language, of course).

TEMPERATURE

No geranium (excluding the hardy types) will survive more than an isolated and slight drop below freezing point, whether indoors or out. Apart from that, modern varieties, at least, seem happiest when the variation in temperatures between day and night is at its smallest. In normal growing conditions it is therefore preferable to keep night temperatures as high as possible, but not higher than day temperatures, and day temperatures as low as possible.

Extreme variations in temperature are as likely to cause reddening discolouration of leaves, as are cold temperatures on their own. This reddening effect is not in itself harmful to the plant and there is no immediate necessity to remove the affected leaves. Indeed, the red leaves seem to serve no purpose, good or bad, other than being a form of communication to the grower, telling him to increase the night temperature and/or lower the day temperature. Basic temperature control is best left to one of the various automatic devices which are now available to the greenhouse owner. These include thermostats for bringing heating into operation and switching it off again when the desired temperature is achieved and also the automatic temperature-controlled ventilation devices that open and close windows according to greenhouse temperature. The grower merely has to decide the temperature at which to set the devices to come into operation. The cost of heating alone usually determines the minimum night temperature and geraniums will survive happily, but make little growth, if this is maintained at between 35°F (2°C) and 40°F (4°C). The lower the night temperature, the lower the day temperature should be, so that the temptation to warm up the greenhouse during the day is to be avoided at all costs, and the ventilators should be opened as soon as the normal maximum night temperature is reached. Equally, during winter months it is advisable to conserve as much natural heat as possible so that once the outside temperature begins to fall ventilators can be closed.

Some slight ventilation must be maintained at all times when heating is in operation and it is usual to leave one roof-vent open about half an inch throughout the winter for this purpose. Paraffin heaters are not, of course, usually used with automatic temperature control, and as they create a damper environment than most other forms of heat, ventilation is even more important with them—especially as geraniums object strongly to undissipated paraffin fumes. During the late autumn and spring periods, when those who do not have fully automatic heating systems are tempted to discontinue (or delay starting) night heating, newspapers spread across the top of plants overnight will usually protect them from snap frosts. This method can also be used in cold frames before geraniums are brought in during autumn or after they have been put out in the spring. If you don't wish to trust your instinct as to when this precaution is necessary, the local weather forecast, available from the GPO in Britain, can be most useful: for the price of a local off-peak telephone call you can hear what minimum night temperature is expected in your particular locality. Local radio stations sometimes give this information but seldom in as much detail as the telephone service.

Winter temperature can be preserved by lining the greenhouse with polythene sheets which create a double-glazing effect, reducing temperature variations. Do not, of course, obstruct the ventilators, as no amount of heat conservation justifies lack of ventilation.

YELLOW LEAVES

Perhaps the most common problem experienced by beginners to geranium growing is yellowing of the lower leaves of plants. It is certainly the problem most frequently raised with so-called experts, and as the full answer is designed to make the expert appear a charlatan it is as unpopular as it is tedious.

The reasons why leaves turn yellow are not only numerous but a succession of opposites; when the various possibilities are listed, beginners are often left as wise as they were before they asked the question. The only way to obtain a really helpful answer is to produce a plant for diagnosis and even that may not give the experts all the information they need.

Firstly, however, it is necessary to point out that there may be no problem at all, as more geranium leaves turn yellow as a result of old age than any other cause. No leaf arrives with an everlasting guarantee or even a twelve-month warranty. In fact any six-month-old leaf has served the plant well and is entitled to be thinking of a decent burial on the compost heap. Such leaves, however, usually have a healthy look about them, apart from their colour, almost until the end and cause no harm to the plant. Another cause, in some varieties more than others, is the virtual exclusion of light from the leaves affected due to the very close proximity of surrounding leaves, and here again there is nothing constructive a grower can do about it, other than trying to open up the plant by staking stems further apart.

Some leaves turn yellow before their predecessors, when a shoot is developing from that particular leaf joint, almost as if the plant has decided to abandon the leaf and devote all its energies to the new shoot. It is then just as well to give the plant what it wants and remove the offending leaf. One well-known exhibitor actually removes such leaves as soon as shoots begin to appear, to force the plant to concentrate on the new stem, whether or not the leaf is showing signs of yellowing.

Other causes of yellow leaves are bad news and often result from one of the extremes of normal cultivation conditions. Underwatering and overwatering are examples of this, as both cause lower leaves to become yellow. Overwatering has been dealt with at some length previously, but underwatering produces a similar effect, although the lower leaves are normally crisper than on overwatered plants. In both cases the yellow leaves should be removed immediately (they will never revert to green) and, whenever possible, each stem should be stopped to promote side shoots. Underwatered plants should be left to stand in a container of water for as long as is necessary for the compost to become completely saturated, after which the pot can be removed, allowed to drain, and subsequently watered normally, taking care not to over-correct and water again too soon.

Draughts and lack of ventilation will also both cause leaves to yellow, and the cures are obvious. Perhaps the most rapid change in leaf colour from green to yellow occurs when a paraffin heater is used without adequate ventilation (a couple of windows opened at least an inch is all that is necessary to prevent this occurring).

Too little or too much fertilizer can cause leaves to yellow, as will a lack of trace elements; this often occurs when a plant is left in the same compost too long. All are simply corrected, the first two by adjusting the quantity of fertilizer (you will normally know better than anyone if you have been guilty of applying too much or too little) and the last by repotting into a larger pot or bedding the plant out in the garden.

Bedding a plant into the garden during the summer can be an excellent 'cure-all' technique and can save considerable time spent fussing over an ailing plant trying to right the wrongs you have perpetrated upon it.

GREENHOUSE LAYOUT AND USES

The relative merits of different greenhouses, lean-tos and conservatories, their shape, construction or situation, are a subject on their own. The advice applicable here is firstly to read one or more of the excellent books available *before* buying a new greenhouse (or building one yourself) and, secondly, always to buy one bigger than you think you will need—even then you'll find it won't be big enough! Staging within the selected greenhouse, however, can be important to the cultivation of geraniums. If you are not fortunate enough to have a garden or potting shed near your greenhouse, it is best to allocate a small section as a working area with a sturdy bench. A formica or similar top to the bench is well worthwhile as it can frequently be washed down with a suitable disinfectant to reduce the risk of spreading or encouraging disease. The width of your greenhouse will usually dictate the width of the staging. As the wider a bench is the more difficult it becomes to water the plants nearest the glass without splashing others, and the narrower the aisle(s) the more likely you are to knock and damage plants, do not opt for excessively wide staging.

Arrange your plants in approximate increasing heights, the lowest at the south-facing side ranging to the tallest at the northerly side. This prevents smaller plants becoming leggy in the search for light when grown in the shade of a larger plant. Unfortunately this arrangement can cause difficulty in attending to smaller plants, when larger plants are between you and them, so it is best to group each size together but from the glass to the inside edge of the bench, the south-east aspect of the greenhouse usually proving the most suitable and convenient position for the smallest plants.

Ideally, plants should not be grown below other plants as, apart from the obvious shading this creates, on all but the north side, plants above and below normal bench height are much more difficult to attend to. Water is likely to splash or drip on to plants below even if the plants themselves don't fall on to their downstairs neighbour. However, this is not always practical at all times of year and if perfection is not possible, southerly ground levels and northerly shelves should be filled first. Tiered staging, particularly on the northerly side, can often be put to good use, although it can be restrictive both as regards width, which if just right one month will be too narrow the next, and height, especially as the tiering approaches the eaves. It is often more convenient to achieve the same effect by standing plants on upturned pots; this is a more flexible (if precarious) alternative to fixed tiering.

Finally, one excellent piece of advice, seldom achieved but worth aiming for, is to go into the winter with your greenhouse half-empty—by late spring the plants will have more than taken up the spare space as they have developed.

CLEANLINESS

Prevention being better than cure, it is always worth keeping your greenhouse, pots and tools as clean as possible. Once every year the interior of the greenhouse should be thoroughly sprayed and wiped down with disinfectant and you need look no further than Jeyes Fluid which is also excellent for cleaning pots. Never re-use a pot without cleaning it thoroughly first— it isn't a big job if you can convince your husband or wife how essential it is!

ENJOYMENT

Never forget that gardening in general, and geranium growing in particular, should be an enjoyable relaxing hobby. When you find yourself putting off until tomorrow what you should have done yesterday, then immediately reduce the number of plants you are growing. You and the remaining plants will be all the better for it.

5 Growing a Well-shaped Plant

Apart from bringing up children, there can be few things more satisfying than producing a well-grown plant from a cutting or seed and seeing it achieve its full glory. This applies whether the plant is a permanent garden feature such as a shrub or tree, a garden annual or an indoor plant raised in the house or greenhouse.

The indoor plants perhaps present the greatest challenge to the grower as they are in an unnatural environment and consequently demand a greater personal commitment, so that by the time they reach maturity they are virtually 'one of the family'. Geraniums, whether grown for the garden or indoors, must spend many months under your constant care, and they repay you most beautifully and for much longer than most other flowering plants. To achieve their full potential, however, they do require a little more than the occasional larger pot with fresh compost and the usual regular watering and feeding.

This chapter is concerned with the finer points that give your geranium plants the opportunity to surpass themselves and thereby give you the greatest personal satisfaction from their performance. The genuine pleasure given you by a pot plant purchased when in flower pales into insignificance when you have a plant you have nurtured yourself from seed or cutting. Similarly, plants you have grown for bedding purposes from seed or cuttings always appear better than those your neighbour has bought from a nearby garden centre and planted straight out. A few techniques discussed here help you to ensure that your plants not only look better to you but to your neighbour as well—and that's the real test!

STOPPING
As mentioned in our final 'golden rule' (Chapter 4), removing

the growing point or tip of each stem is an essential part of good geranium culture, probably *the* most essential. This operation, generally referred to as 'stopping', is a common enough procedure with many plants, as any fuchsia or chrysanthemum grower will know. It serves two very distinct purposes, however, and one should not be confused with the other: these are shaping and timing, and it is the former that we are most concerned with in this chapter. Timing (or the finer points thereof) is more the prerogative of exhibitors, who are honoured with a couple of chapters all to themselves later in the book.

As most plants, the geranium requires a good basic framework of stems if it is to develop into a well-shaped plant. Unfortunately, it is not consistent in its branching, unlike a fuchsia which is uniform and accommodating when stopped correctly. Anyone who has pruned a rose bush carefully to outward-facing eyes, only to find the strongest shoot forms below and grows inward, will know what to expect from geraniums.

The first stop is the most important and should be carried out as early as possible in a plant's life-cycle. Sometimes nature will have taken a hand at the cutting stage, especially if you have neglected it while it was rooting, in that the growing tip may have dried out and failed to develop. This need cause no concern as you would have done something similar to the plant if it had not happened. Provided the cutting is growing steadily and appears to have settled happily into its (first) intermediate pot, you should remove the growing tip yourself, normally within a couple of weeks of putting it into that pot. The easiest way of removing a tip is to use a short length of thin split cane sharpened to a point. This can be inserted close to the growing point, which may be anything from a pinhead in size, still covered by unopened stipules, or a small developing leaf clear of the now-opened stipules, and by exerting slight pressure the tip will break cleanly away—it almost 'pops' off. The object is to remove the tip immediately above the preceding leaf or leaves and as close to them as possible. It is almost impossible not to achieve this with the pinhead-size growing point, but once the leaf has begun to open you can usually see where to apply the point of the cane—between the base of the opening stipules and above the leaf joint below.

Ideally, this all-important first stop should have been carried out before the basic type (size) plant has reached 3 inches in height from compost level (2 in for a dwarf and $1\frac{1}{2}$ in for a miniature). This ensures that the stem produces side shoots and that those shoots are as close to the base of the plant as possible, so avoiding the all-too-common, unsightly space between the pot and the plant proper as it develops. A well-grown geranium will have leaves down to the pot rim throughout twelve months of growing, if correctly treated.

Having performed this initial stop there is nothing you can do (except hope and pray) to encourage the plant to develop the three or four side shoots that will make future training and shaping so much simpler. After two or three weeks you will have a good idea if you have been lucky or not, as one or more small side shoots will have begun to develop. If, at this point, only one shoot has appeared it should be stopped again immediately, or as soon as it is possible to attack the growing point with your sharpened cane, hopefully forcing other shoots to develop. Equally, if more than one shoot has appeared, but one—usually the one nearest the top of the plant—is racing away to the apparent detriment of the other, or others, the vigorous one should be stopped to allow the smaller ones to establish themselves. Seedlings tend to produce side shoots more abundantly and uniformly than the average cutting and for them the second 'initial' stop just mentioned is seldom necessary.

Within six to ten weeks (depending on the season of the year and the temperature the plant is growing in) of the first stop, the resulting stems should have developed three or four leaf joints and each stem may now be stopped again. The stems of a basic type should be between 2 and 3 in long for this second stop (proportionately shorter for a dwarf or miniature) and at that length the second method of improving the shape of the plant can begin to be applied.

STAKING OR TYING
This involves staking or tying the developing stems as evenly apart as possible to provide a uniform framework of stems on which the following stems can develop the bushy plant you are seeking. At this stage the stems have not begun to harden and can gradually be drawn to the desired position. This can be achieved in one of two ways depending on the situation of the developing stems. The simplest method is to draw two stems towards each other by use of twine, raffia or 'twist-it' ties. Never

apply too much pressure at this stage but merely move the stems slightly towards each other, returning every week or fortnight to shorten the tie so that they gradually assume the position you desire. This method is, of course, suitable only when both stems are in the wrong position initially, although it is sometimes possible to 'move' one further than the other by tying it nearer its growing tip, the tie for the other being put nearer the point at which it breaks from the main stem.

However, the most satisfactory method of training stems is to insert a short split cane at the point where you desire the stem to grow and tie the stem to it, or as close to it as possible, again drawing it closer each week by shortening the tie when necessary. This staking has to be used when a single stem requires moving (its neighbours being suitably placed). It has the added advantage that outward-growing stems can also be trained more horizontally, which serves to keep subsequent side shoots lower on the plant, giving it a wider appearance as well as keeping the leaves lower on the plant. Do not make the mistake of tying all the stems outward as it is essential that at least one grows upwards centrally within the outer stems if all the flowerheads are not to appear around the edge of the plant.

During this early period it is important that the individual plants have adequate clear space around them and are turned regularly to ensure they are able to grow freely. It may be necessary, as further new stems begin to develop, to remove some of the older leaves if they are inhibiting the growth or direction of growth of the stems. Also, if there were too few original side shoots (four or more are really needed) to form an adequate framework, some of these new stems may have to be tied into position to fill in any spaces left by the inadequacies of the original breaks. Otherwise, given a good initial framework, subsequent shoots should have sufficient space between them to develop separate from each other into a naturally bushy shape; so that with luck all 'work' to train the plant will have been completed within the first three months of the date on which the cutting was taken.

The regular routine inspections of the plant should thereafter be sufficient to alert you to any stem growing too vigorously (a quick stop within two or three weeks of it developing will correct) or in an unwanted position (tie it into a more suitable position or remove it completely if necessary). Already you have done all the training and shaping that should be necessary before flowering for bedding plants and pot plants alike, although most exhibitors, seeking after perfection, will try to perform one or two more stops on every stem to make the plant more compact and bushier.

TIMING

Whether you are satisfied with just these first and second stops or decide to perform a further stop, you will have to apply a little of that forethought mentioned in an earlier chapter. While the more critical timing so necessary to exhibitors need not concern those who are merely growing geraniums to decorate their gardens, homes and greenhouses, the basic principles are worth considering. Stopping a stem obviously prevents that stem from developing flowers, and in approximate terms the following side shoots will require about twelve weeks to reach the point when they are proudly displaying their first flower. It therefore follows that all your bedding geraniums should have their final stop at about the same time (within a week of each other) if they are to be in an equal stage of development when planted out—they certainly look better that way.

Assuming you like your bedders to be bearing their first flowers when planted out, the final stop should have been performed some twelve weeks earlier. As they cannot go outside until you are reasonably sure that frosts have finished, your particular planting-out date will depend on your experience of your individual locality. If however we assume that, for UK growers, the second week in May is safe enough, the final stop should have been carried out in the third week of February. But if you have taken the original cuttings at the beginning of September as suggested in an earlier chapter, and then performed the first stop some six weeks later as you really should, you have some sixteen or seventeen weeks between first and second stop. That is really too long, so that unless you can plant out earlier than the second week in May and take your cuttings later than early September, you really have no alternative but to stop the plant again before the second week in December. If you leave the second stop much later than that, the new stems may not have made sufficient growth (at that time of year) to be of ideal length for the final stop.

Incidentally if the weather has been sneaky and delivers a

late frost after you have planted your bedders into the garden, you can sometimes prevent damage to them by soaking the foliage with cold water from a watering can or garden hose before the sun gets on them. It doesn't do much for the flowers of course, but it might save the plant (if the frost wasn't too hard) and it probably justifies having a late breakfast on the few occasions it happens in a lifetime.

Pot plants for decoration are a different matter, of course, as probably the last thing you want is for every geranium plant you possess to burst into flower on the same day. They would never actually do that, but to have every plant in bloom with five or six months of the warmer weather still to come borders on the extravagant and is unnecessary to say the least. You can consider staggering the final stop for such plants over a two-month period so that different plants are coming into flower progressively from about April onwards. While most zonals do not respond very well to being brought into flower too early in the year, most regals are quite happy to oblige from about that time of year, and some will even flower for Mothering Sunday (mid-March) if you talk to them nicely (and choose the right varieties, of course).

Let the regals have their heads early in the season, as they are in any event more difficult to grow to perfection as the summer progresses—not impossible, just more difficult. Regals will break naturally, without stopping, if left to their own dev-ices, but it does no harm to encourage them with the usual initial stop after six weeks from taking the cutting and then another final stop some time in January, to bring them into flower from April onwards. A final stop in February will pro-duce May regals and so on. If regals are required later in the summer it is preferable to take cuttings early in the year (about seven months before flowering) and leave them to develop naturally after the initial stop has been performed. Some var-ieties, such as 'Hazel Harmony', respond very well to this method; so experiment a little.

As in the case of regals some dwarf zonals, 'Morval' for example, are best grown from cuttings taken about six months previously if required to flower late summer into autumn.

All this timing nonsense, sheer oversight on your part, uneven growth of one stem and many other reasons will almost certainly mean that on several occasions during a year a stop will be unsuitable because the stem(s) will have grown on too far. There is nothing unusual in this—even the most fastidious exhibitor frequently meets this problem. It merely requires that the stem(s) must be cut back to a more suitable length rather than merely removing the growing point. However, it is always preferable, but not always possible, that such cut backs crop up not at the final stopping but on an earlier occasion.

The final stop should always be carried out to every possible shoot even if it has only a couple of leaves as, if small stems are left to grow on at this time, they will almost certainly develop more rapidly and come into flower as much as four weeks before the rest of the stems. To avoid this, it is best to allow at least eight weeks between the next to last stop and the final stop, so that the shoots that develop are a reasonable length when the final stop is required.

Zonals can be brought into flower in the house or greenhouse quite reasonably from the end of April onwards, the single-flowered varieties being happier that early in the year than the doubles, which are normally at their best from the second half of June until well into the autumn. These natural preferences are well worth considering when staggering the dates of intermediate and final stopping.

USING A GROWTH REGULATOR

Most gardeners will be familiar with the beautiful pots of dwarf chrysanthemums available from florists and garden centres and will also know that if planted out in the garden after flowering they revert to a more natural chrysanthemum habit. They are, of course, not really dwarf varieties but are chemically treated to inhibit their upward growth. There are several such concoctions but the only one universally recommended for geraniums at this time is Cycocel (CCC). It can be applied as a soil drench or as a foliar spray and while the latter method is preferred by commercial growers (for whom it is really intended) with their large numbers of plants, watering into the pots is undoubtedly better for the amateur, although it does take considerably longer.

Firstly, it should be stressed that because plants are grown

Ivy-leaved geranium 'Sugar Baby', of dwarf habit, excellent for greenhouse or show (*Garden News*)

over a longer period by amateurs, so that more stopping opportunities are available to them, equally compact bushy plants can be grown without using Cycocel. Commercial geraniums can be sold in flower from mid-May from F1 seed sown four months earlier, but very few amateurs would enjoy such production-line techniques, nor the heating costs involved.

However, apart from earlier flowering, the claims for Cycocel treatment include more pronounced zoning, more compact growth and increased basal shoots, and it is this latter aspect that almost certainly interests the few amateurs who have been tempted to invest in Cycocel—to say it isn't cheap would be putting it mildly! The most common concentration of Cycocel available (most UK Chempak stockists have it on hand or will obtain it for you) is 40 per cent in solution, and this must be considerably diluted before applying it to your plants.

The dilution rate is 4.5 cc of the solution in 1 litre of water (0.7 fl oz per gallon) and this resulting mixture is applied to each plant pot, just before it requires watering, in the following quantities: 1 fl oz to a $2\frac{1}{2}$ in pot, 2 fl oz to a 3 in pot and 3 fl oz a $3\frac{1}{2}$ in pot. Only the first intermediate pot sizes are shown, as the growth regulator is best applied at that stage, after the plants have been in those pots five or six weeks and have been initially stopped. Commercial growers seldom stop their plants, relying on growth regulators only to provide the compact bushy plants they desire. Should you be so bone-idle that you are tempted to take the easy, quick way and spray, be warned not to if the night temperature is likely to fall below 50°F (10°C), or in bright sunny weather, and don't water for a couple of days after spraying to give the plants time to absorb the Cycocel. Spray until the liquid is dripping off the leaves and don't panic when, about a week after spraying, the leaves start to yellow at the edges—it soon disappears. The addition of a small amount of a suitable spreader, such as Agral, to the spray solution is recommended (about 1 cc a litre should suffice).

STOPPING WHEN IN FLOWER

Having achieved something approaching a well-shaped plant in flower it would be a shame now to allow it to run amok and

(*above*) 'Deacon Lilac Mist', most popular of the 'Deacon' varieties, showing the small, compact plant with an abundance of blooms. (*below*) Undoubtedly the most popular tricolour zonal 'Henry Cox'

become misshapen and leggy, as most varieties certainly will if you let them. Regals, apart from the 'continuous-flowering' varieties, are perhaps an exception, in that they will bloom for a limited period and then take a rest. As soon as they finish flowering all the flowering stems should be cut out, leaving new shoots to develop and flower about ten weeks later.

Zonals, ivies and most of the species and scented varieties will remain in good shape and condition much longer if some judicious stopping or pruning is carried out while the plant is flowering. Most geraniums extend their internodal length once they begin to flower so that unless some continuous attention is given they soon lose their compact bushy appearance.

This tendency can quite easily be curtailed, however, if each stem is stopped after it has produced two or three flowers. As plants come into flower they can be left for about four weeks (they are probably never better than during the six weeks after they first begin to flower) after which time the longest stems, about half of those on the plant, should be stopped by removing the growing point from between the last formed double-leaf joint. This should mean that you are stopping only stems which have produced at least one flowerhead with another well on the way to flowering and perhaps even another bud developing happily at the joint below the stop.

As already mentioned in the chapter on the geranium's normal growing habit, a side shoot should be developing quite vigorously from the joint below the first flower and it is this that we are trying to encourage to produce flowers. Actually other side shoots below and above this principal shoot will also develop more vigorously once the stem has been stopped, producing even greater flowering potential.

After another three or four weeks the remaining stems should now be the longest on the plant and may then be stopped in turn. This process will not have reduced the number of flowers on the plant for at least the first seven weeks of blooming and, surprisingly perhaps, reduces the number of flowers produced over three months by only 10 per cent, a small price to pay for retaining an attractive well-shaped plant throughout the flowering season.

To summarise this 'in-flower stopping': two flowers to each stem are normally sufficient for most varieties, but the stopping of flowering stems should be staggered so that at least half the stems are growing on and developing buds at all times. Such stopping should be evenly distributed around the plant; if all the longest stems are on one side it is wiser to leave one or two for a couple of weeks to ensure an even distribution of flowers.

Even bedding geraniums and trailing ivy-leaved plants outdoors should be treated this way, except perhaps some of the dwarf varieties which remain quite compact outdoors even when flowering freely. The job is quite easily and quickly done when removing the dead flowerheads, as you must, to prevent their rotting back and causing stem damage.

Houseplants that have been grown to flowering in the greenhouse and then brought into the house should be treated similarly but returned to the greenhouse (to freshen up) after about six weeks. If you have staggered your final stopping as suggested previously a replacement plant that has been in flower for a week or two should be available and after that has been indoors for about six weeks the original plant should have recuperated sufficiently to pay a return visit.

It should not be assumed from the length of this chapter that stopping is a time-consuming or difficult process—it isn't. Ten minutes to each plant spread over a whole year should be more than enough once you have got the hang of it, and you will spend a lot longer than that just watering a plant in the course of a year.

SECOND-YEAR PLANTS

To suggest to some keen growers that a fully grown geranium can be successfully kept through the winter and the following spring and summer, as bedder or as pot plant, is to invite ridicule. These people do of course have a point, in that the vast majority of varieties can be grown to their full potential within a twelve-month period, provided the last three or four months are summer ones. However, that does not alter the fact that the remaining minority of varieties can be better plants when grown into the second year; nor does it admit that with proper treatment many plants of the majority of varieties will, to outward appearances, be just as good the second summer as they were in their first. They may lack just a little vigour and freshness the second time around, but they can more than make up for this with a better, more compact shape and more blooms.

Second-year plants almost without exception will have

smaller leaves, but this can be an advantage with some varieties which have very large leaves, overpowering to both the onlooker and the plant itself in the vigour of its first-year youth. Flowerheads too may be slightly smaller in the second year, but as they are normally more prolific numerically, the overall effect can be equally pleasing.

BEDDERS

The bedders are simple and convenient as second year plants, given enough space to accommodate them in a greenhouse until late spring the following year. If the plant has been grown in a pot the first year it will make an ideal specimen bedding plant the next summer if all the stems are cut back (pruned) to about 3 inches in length about mid-September. After cutting back to immediately above a leaf joint, each cut should be dusted with a sulphur powder to prevent rot. The pot should not be watered for at least seven days and then after being given a good water and feed it may be stood outside in a cold frame or sunk to about half the pot depth in the garden. It can normally be left in its existing pot until bedded out the following spring

If the plant you wish to grow on as a bedder next year is already bedded out in the garden, it should be cut back and dusted as if in a pot, and then lifted after about three weeks when the new growth has begun to develop. Most of the soil should be removed from around the roots which should then be trimmed with scissors to about 3 inches in length. It can then usually be potted into a 5 in pot and treated similarly to cutback pot plants. When frosts become likely it should be moved into the greenhouse and watered and fertilized as you would a first-year plant.

At the end of January all the new stems should be cut back or stopped at a reasonable length and then allowed to grow unhindered until it is time to harden them off in a cold frame two or three weeks before bedding out. Once planted into the garden they will make very rapid growth and, due to the greater number of stems, will invariably spread outwards more than first-year bedding varieties do, so give them plenty of room all round.

POT PLANTS

Geraniums that are to be grown as pot plants for a second year are treated a little differently, in that after cutting back and dusting in September they should be knocked out of their existing pots and as much of the old soil as possible should be teased away. This will inevitably cause some root damage, but as the roots are to be trimmed to between 2 and 3 in this is not too serious. If the plants have been left without water for at least seven days before removing from their pots you will find the compost breaks away more easily. After most of the soil has been removed and the roots trimmed, the plant should be repotted in a 1 in smaller pot than you intend as the final pot, and left there to recover and grow on until the time you would normally move a first-year plant into its final pot (five or six months before flowering).

Once the plant has become established in its first pot after repotting (normally four to six weeks) it is worth spending some time tying the stems into an even framework, each stem equidistant from its neighbour and as horizontal as possible. At this time of year most varieties are inclined to produce side shoots with great gusto and it may even be necessary to rub off some of the less vigorous, particularly towards the centre of the plant, if they appear too congested.

As soon as the side shoots are growing strongly the plant should be treated in all respects as if it were a first-year plant—water and feed as required, turn regularly, stop as frequently as possible and give plenty of space and light. Second-year plants will always perform better indoors in the early part of the summer and you should therefore stop them for early-season flowering rather than try to carry them through to late summer. First-year plants are much more suitable for late flowering.

Inevitably, some varieties do not respond well to such treatment and some require more attention than others. Miniature and many dwarf varieties are less successful than basic varieties, but most basic-type varieties, whether zonal, regal, ivy-leaf or species, respond well. Those that respond better than most when grown on a second year are most species, scented-leaf types, strong-growing basic zonals (especially tricolours) and the more vigorous ivy-leaf and hybrid ivy-leaf types.

THE 16-MONTH GROWING PROGRAMME
There is another, more satisfactory, method of growing plants for more than twelve months and there are virtually no excep-

tions to this method. This involves early-season cuttings taken from February to April, which are grown on steadily, stopping only, without cutting back at any time, for about 16 months before being allowed to flower. Obviously, with stops being given for at least 12 months, such plants become very compact and bushy, even when their normal tendency is towards an open, leggy habit. The disadvantages are obvious: they require a great deal more attention and take up valuable space. The resultant plant, however, is more often than not well worth the extra effort. As it is preferable to retain the plant in its (final) intermediate pot for the additional time it is growing, so that it spends only six months in its final pot, particular attention must be given during that intermediate-pot stage to watering and feeding; use a high-nitrogen fertilizer until the plant is ready to flower. Such plants should always be flowered in their maximum pot size—don't restrict a basic zonal to a 5 in pot but make sure its final one is at least 6 in.

Plant types that generally respond well to this sixteen month growing programme are the low-growing miniature zonals, the less compact dwarf zonals, regals, ivy-leaved, the strong leggy basic zonals, including bicolour and tricolour-leaved varieties and many species and scented-leaved.

This method is very much a compromise between using genuine second-year plants, which have been grown through two winters and survived a hard cut back and possibly root pruning, and the more usual ten-to-twelve-month-old plants. It is certainly worth trying three or four suitable plants by each method so that you can judge the results for yourself. The method described above will certainly produce a better-shaped plant than a twelve-month one if normal stopping routine has been followed when necessary.

6 A Geranium Calendar—and Keeping Records

The following suggestions of appropriate jobs for the geranium grower to do at various times of the year must be subject to various qualifications. It is, of course, a British calendar, and as even that can differ by as much as four weeks between south-west England and north-east Scotland, a rough attempt to average out that variation to what is probably right for an inland area somewhere around York has been made.

To clarify any adjustment that individual readers may wish to make to the calendar for their particular locality, it is assumed that spring begins in late March, summer in early May, autumn in September and winter in November. It is suprising how little apparently adverse or good weather affects the normal growth of a geranium, either indoors or outside, over a reasonable period of about three months—one week either way is all that might be expected as a variation from the 'norm'.

No detailed timing for exhibitors is included in this calendar, as more specific information is included in two later chapters, intended primarily for exhibitors but possibly of general interest to most growers. However, for more casual supporters of local shows some approximate dates are mentioned assuming the show is in mid-June. These should be adjusted to suit your actual show date.

The correct starting point for a geranium calendar would probably be June or July, when most cuttings begin to be taken, but for the sake of convention we will start in January.

JANUARY
1. Examine plants regularly for dead or dying foliage and even stems, removing immediately any that show the slightest signs of decay. Dust any obvious or possible wounds with sulphur powder.

2. Water and fertilize sparingly unless you are growing at a minimum temperature of 55°F (13°C) or above, when more will be required.

Exhibition plants
Stop all plants and pot-on to the appropriate size final pot.

Greenhouse
Try to open doors and ventilators for at least an hour a day when outside temperatures permit.

Home
Ensure plants receive maximum light but take away from windows each evening.

FEBRUARY
1. and 2. as January, but increase water and feeding gradually.
3. Any of the last season's plants not repotted in September can now be knocked out of their pots and have the soil removed and roots trimmed; repot in the same-size pots.
4. Regals intended for early flowering, and zonals or ivies required for bedding out, should be given a final stop.
5. Cuttings from tricolour zonals appear to develop well if taken now and grown on as sixteen-month plants.

Home and Greenhouse
As in January.

MARCH
1. Cuttings for sixteen-month plants and autumn flowering should be taken as early as possible this month, using bottom heat when available.
2. Pot up tricolour cuttings taken last month.
3. Light spraying can be started this month, and watering and feeding will be more frequently required.
4. Treat all plants with systemic insecticide.
5. Make up hanging baskets.
6. Begin stopping plants required for June-onward flowering— preferably in batches every two weeks.

Cutting back the single-stemmed parent plant. Note the cut is made directly above the upper leaf that is to remain on the plant, leaving excess stem below the 'leaf and flower' joint that will form the basis of the cutting *(Garden News)*

The flower stem has been cut off and the stipules are now being removed *(Garden News)*

A stipule removed from the cutting *(Garden News)*

Removing the lower leaf
(Garden News)

The lower leaf removed from the cutting *(Garden News)*

Trimming the base of the cutting immediately below the lowest joint *(Garden News)*

A further leaf has been removed (one of the pair at the first node above the 'cutting' joint/node) and a last stipule, from the tip of the cutting, is being taken off *(Garden News)*

The cutting being firmed into a Jiffy 7. Roots should be showing within ten to twenty days *(Garden News)*

Exhibition plants

The final stops should begin from the middle of the month onwards until the very end of the month, depending on the particular variety.

Greenhouse

Except on exceptionally cold or warm days you should gradually increase ventilation to four or five hours daily, normally closing down in mid-afternoon.

Home

Plants will now begin to require turning more frequently and will appreciate ventilation whenever possible.

APRIL

1. March cuttings should be potted-on as soon as roots have formed.
2. Continue giving a final stop to plants in batches every two weeks.
3. Continue spraying, including one with Epsom Salts and perhaps one with Maxicrop.
4. Towards the end of the month move bedders into a cold frame to harden off. Cover with newspapers to protect plants when frosts are anticipated. Hanging baskets intended for outdoor display may also be put into a cold frame.
5. All plants should be growing strongly and regular watering with fertilizer will now be necessary.
6. Keep plants well spaced; if not enough room, discard weakest plants or treat as bedders.
7. Change to high-potash feed from second week in month for plants that have had their final stop about two or three weeks previously.

Exhibition plants

Complete final stops in first week of this month.

Greenhouse

Full ventilation should now be possible virtually every day until early evening.

Home

Only those plants intended for early-season flowering indoors need remain; the rest can be put out in a cold greenhouse or frame.

MAY

1. Give final spray with Epsom Salts and then stop spraying as buds begin to appear above the foliage.
2. Plants that have been hardened off can be planted out directly into the garden or into tubs and window boxes, once you are reasonably sure the risk of frost has passed.
3. The final batch of plants should be stopped in the first half of this month.
4. Shade the greenhouse as soon as the buds on the early-flowering plants begin to open.

Exhibition plants

As buds develop make sure they are as evenly spaced as possible by use of ties or stakes.

Greenhouse

Maximum ventilation can now be given at all times and some ventilators left fully open overnight.

Home

As plants come into flower, remember to stop each stem after every second flower to encourage bushier growth and larger flowers.

JUNE

1. Treat all plants (including bedders) with systemic insecticides.
2. Cut back any early-flowering regals that have completed flowering. Plants that were selected as being best for cuttings should be stood out in the fully opened cold frame or a sheltered position, but the remainder may be grown on for a second flush of flowers.
3. All finished blooms should be removed from bedding and indoor plants regularly.
4. While removing the dead flowers remember to carry out the regular stopping of leading stems (after the second or third

blooms) to restrict upward growth and encourage bushier plants.

5. Towards the end of the month begin to take cuttings for next year's plants.

Exhibition plants

Remember to send off entry form (if required). Immediately before the show go over each plant thoroughly, removing any dead or dying stipules, leaves or florets. Any unsightly or obvious stakes and ties should be taken out. Check that the intended exhibit conforms with schedule requirements, eg for pot size or for single or double flowered.

Home

Substitute the earliest-flowering plants with fresh plants from the greenhouse that have just begun to flower.

JULY

1. Continue removing dead flowerheads and routine stopping of leading stems.
2. Cut back remaining regals.
3. Continue to take cuttings from selected stock for next year's plants and pot-on rooted cuttings struck in June, stopping where necessary.
4. Where applicable, pot-on the sixteen-month plants, rooted in March, to their second intermediate pot.
5. All plants intended for flowering next year will benefit from frequent light sprays with clear water, late in the evenings whenever possible.
6. Check that the shading does not require further application or touching up.
7. Sow seed for pot plants required next year.

AUGUST

1. Cuttings for next year's indoor plants should be completed early this month, as well as those from regals cut back in June.
2. Plants that have been flowering for a couple of months will welcome a spell outside in the cold frame or partly sunk into the garden. This should create space for the later-flowering varieties to develop properly.

3. Do not neglect pot plants that have been stood outside; they still require water and feeding.
4. Pot-on rooted cuttings taken in July.
5. Continue spraying next year's plants, including one spray with Epsom Salts.
6. At the end of this month you should start taking cuttings for next year's bedding plants.
7. Prick out seedlings into individual pots and treat as rooted cuttings from then on.

Home
Substitute existing plants for fresh plants from the greenhouse that have just begun to flower, or bring back the plants removed in June which should have freshened up well.

SEPTEMBER
1. Pot-on cuttings taken in August.
2. Take cuttings of plants required for bedding out next year as early in the month as possible.
3. Sow seed for next year's bedding plants.
4. Check that you have cuttings (rooted or rooting) or plants for all varieties that you intend to grow again next year. This is the last really suitable month, before March next year, that cuttings will root happily without bottom heat.
5. Towards the middle of the month stop all plants being grown for pot work next year and discontinue spraying.
6. Outdoor plants and pot plants indoors that you wish to grow on for a second year should be cut back. Allow them to begin to develop new shoots before (a) lifting, trimming roots and potting or boxing; or (b) knocking out of existing pots, trimming roots and potting into the smaller-size pot.
7. Treat all plants with systemic insecticide.
8. Search out any caterpillars, particularly on plants brought in from the garden.
9. Continue to water and feed plants still in flower, but others will not require as much now, except perhaps next year's regals.
10. Towards the end of the month begin to move the larger cuttings, taken in June and early July for next year's pot work, into their second intermediate pot.

Greenhouse

At the beginning of this month, preferably on a fine day, take all plants outside and thoroughly disinfect and wash down the interior of the greenhouse and the staging. Shading can also be removed from the middle of the month.

OCTOBER

1. Continue potting-on July and early August cuttings that require a second intermediate pot.
2. A small quantity of water will continue to be required by all plants.
3. Pot-on cuttings of bedding plants taken in September.
4. Prick out seed sown in September as soon as first leaves have opened. Treat as cuttings of bedders from now on, stopping all plants once they have formed five or six leaves.
5. As this is normally a damp time of year, pay particular attention to removing dying leaves and flowerheads.
6. Continue to pay particular attention to watering as it is very easy to overwater from now on. If in doubt—DON'T.
7. Order any new varieties you require from specialist nurseries.

Greenhouse

1. You will need to reduce full ventilation considerably during this month—three hours a day will be sufficient except on very sunny days. Close ventilators and doors soon after the temperature begins to fall.
2. Be prepared to heat the greenhouse overnight to maintain a minimum temperature between 40° and 45°F (4° and 7°C).
3. Have a good look round the greenhouse and discard any unwanted plants or earmark them for the compost heap as soon as they finish flowering. Unless you have managed to keep a lot of plants in flower your greenhouse should never be less crowded than it is now.

Home

1. Replace the existing plants with any in the greenhouse that appear to have a reasonable flowering period left. You can discontinue stopping the stems now, as the internodal length will be getting shorter even if they are still flowering.
2. If you have an unheated greenhouse you will need to bring in as many small plants as you can accommodate to get them

through the winter. Try to keep them away from rooms that have gas fires or stoves.

NOVEMBER

1. Stop all pot plants early in the month.
2. Continue to pay particular attention to dying leaves, making sure that none is allowed to rot down on the surface of the compost.

Greenhouse

1. Try to maintain maximum ventilation for a couple of hours a day whenever the outside temperature permits.
2. Heating will probably be required most nights now. If paraffin is being used remember to leave a couple of ventilators slightly open.
3. If you are going to line your greenhouse with polythene this is the month when it should be done.

DECEMBER

1. Try and give the young bedding plants another stop early this month.
2. The sixteen-month plants may be moved into their final pots towards the end of the month, but don't be tempted to over-water them.
3. Treat all plants with systemic insecticide.
4. Catch up on your records (see below) and some geranium reading.

KEEPING RECORDS

The list above must, by necessity, be generalized, showing recommended jobs at approximate times of the year. So don't take everything in it as infallible. It has been frequently stressed that geraniums consist of a mass of exceptions, so that the calendar ideas are really no more than guiding pegs on which to hang the exceptions. Equally, it is not possible in a single volume to refer to exceptions in anything but the widest possible terms, as every exception begets its own exceptions and part of the enjoyment of growing geraniums is in discovering them for yourself.

Remembering exceptions from one year to the next and correctly adjusting your growing pattern to allow for them does really require you to make a few notes when you spot something unusual. Not that a single year is sufficient, generally, clearly to establish the full effect of most exceptions. Having spotted an apparent variation in growing habit you should alter your technique slightly the following year in an endeavour to exaggerate the difference or compensate for it—but keep a brief note of the variations you have made. It can be frustrating if you achieve a particular objective but then realize you are unlikely to be able to repeat it the following year because you can't remember how you did it.

For example, if you grow the regal 'Confetti' and treat all your regals identically, one year, you will usually find that a plant of 'Confetti' will be in full flower about two weeks before most of its companions. You now have a few alternative courses available with this variety the following year. Should you take advantage of your suspicion that you have discovered a naturally early-flowering variety and try to bring the flowering even further forward by taking 'Confetti' cuttings two or three weeks earlier than usual and maintaining this differential throughout its growth, in the hope that you will have it in flower a month or so before other regals? Or do you decide that two weeks ahead of the others suits you fine and try to repeat the same thing the following year? Or even decide that such early flowering is a nuisance and try to delay the flowering the following year by taking cuttings a couple of weeks later than normal?

You may, of course, feel that you can achieve either even earlier flowering or delayed flowering by merely adjusting the date of the last stop, making it two weeks earlier or later. In any event you may wish to do something different from normal, even if it is only to record during another year that 'Confetti' really does flower earlier than other similar plants and to determine more exactly the actual difference.

Equally you may decide to investigate the apparent difference more fully and grow half a dozen plants with different techniques to see if you can establish a common pattern. Incidentally if you do attempt this, half a dozen plants may not be sufficient as it is really necessary to grow at least three plants similarly to establish a 'norm' and you must always grow the same number as a 'control batch' so that you can establish the true variance from basic anticipated performance.

Do avoid using moveable feasts, such as the Easter holidays, as a base for any of your records, as these can vary by several weeks over the years; the actual day and the month will always prove the most reliable reference.

Of course, early flowering is only one of many possible variations you may wish to compensate for. You may wish to try some plants in John Innes compost because they appear too lush in your usual soilless compost, or try others as sixteen-month plants because they make insufficient growth during a normal twelve-month period. Brief permanent notes should be kept of all such experiments, with a record of the success or failure, so that you can repeat, discard or adapt the procedure the following year.

It only remains to warn against trying to keep too many records at one time. Certainly, while you are just beginning to keep records one or two experiments a year will be quite enough to keep you busy and provide additional interest and knowledge. Once you have established a system that is both simple and quick it can be extended as much as you wish, but never let these records interfere more than is absolutely necessary with the important things, such as keeping to the ten golden rules, as that would be self-defeating.

(*above*) Show plant of 'Hazel Cherry', a compact, sturdy regal (*John Keay*) (*below*) An immaculately grown show plant of 'Lady Plymouth', a rose-scented, variegated-leaved form of '*P. Graveolens*'

British and European
Geranium Society

Variety HAZEL CHERRY

7 Exhibiting: the Requirements

Virtually all growers like to show their geraniums. It would be very unusual indeed if you were to visit the home of a fellow geranium-grower and not be invited to look at his plants. There is nothing unusual in that; the same thing would happen between fellow dog-breeders, do-it-yourself home-improvement buffs or tomato-growers. To want to share your hobby with another is not taking an ego trip or letting suppressed latent pride burst forth. It is far more likely to be a sympathetic development of a human relationship totally unconnected with geraniums, dogs, wallpapers or tomatoes.

The showman or exhibitor, as we know him or her, is almost certainly someone who feels strongly that the combination of plants and people is there to be enjoyed and developed. They are usually, though not necessarily, those of us with a strong competitive instinct and probably with an extrovert character, and if all such characteristics were channelled through flower shows, preferably geranium classes, the world would certainly be a better place to live in—even if we couldn't move for all the big beautiful geraniums. Obviously, the competitive instinct is stronger with some exhibitors than others, but it is normally associated with the wish to assess or measure achievements. And the old adage that a successful show is measured not by the quality of the winners but by the quality of the losers could not be more true.

In short, exhibitors are ordinary people with ordinary feelings and the following pages will hopefully encourage a few more growers to venture forth with their geraniums—they will certainly meet some friendly, charming people and may even be

'Highfields Festival', a semi-double flowered zonal, with stakes positioning blooms for exhibition

pleasantly surprised at the standard their plants have achieved. However, the real purpose of these chapters is to explain the standards by which geraniums are assessed and hopefully give you the encouragement and know-how to grow plants that compare favourably with the best in the land—whether you intend to show them to thousands of visitors at Southport Flower Show or to your mother-in-law in the privacy of your own greenhouse.

Unfortunately, the standards by which geraniums are judged are confused by the existence of at least four different sets of 'rules' from four different societies, the Royal Horticultural Society (RHS), the International Geranium Society (IGS —based in the USA), the British Pelargonium and Geranium Society (BPGS) and the British and European Geranium Society (BEGS).

For the purposes of this book the BEGS 'rules' will be used as the basis, for no other reason than that they are, when read on their own and especially when read in conjunction with the accompanying explanations, the most detailed of the four available. They are also the most recently prepared, so most in line with modern practice.

Fortunately, the three specialist societies follow almost identical general principles and are virtually of one mind as to what is and is not desirable in a specimen geranium plant. While BPGS have followed a marking or pointing system based on a 20-point maximum similar to the RHS, BEGS admit that they follow the IGS 100-point maximum system, finding it more manageable and easily explained than the narrower, more critical, band provided by the 20-point system.

The BEGS alone do state quite clearly that final results are arrived at by assuming each plant starts with the maximum 100 points, and points are then deducted for faults under the various aspects listed. The others suggest, somewhat vaguely, that points are 'allocated' after considering meritorious and defective features—a sort of give-and-take operation, which while it works satisfactorily when applied by an experienced judge, can be difficult to explain clearly to an enquiring exhibitor, particularly a beginner.

The actual points structure we are considering is:

CLASSIFICATION

QUALITIES	Zonal Regal Ivy	Bicolour Tricolour (zonals)	Bicolour (ivy)	Scented species	Cut blooms
Cultural quality	30	30	30	50	30
Foliage	15	45	30	30	—
Flowerheads	45	15	30	10	—
Staging & display	10	10	10	10	10
Form & colour	—	—	—	—	60
Uniformity/effect	10 per plant/bloom (groups)				
Total	100 (single)				
	110 (part group)				

While others subdivide the Flowerheads section above by adding 'Pip' and 'Colour', the overall result is similar, although 'Staging and Display' is not consistently mentioned by others unless a group (more than one) or collection of plants is displayed, when a larger proportion of the available points are given over to this aspect.

One area of difference is the BPGS interpretation of ornamental-leaved zonals (which they refer to as 'coloured' or sometimes 'variegated'), because although they do not apparently actually say so, they have included golden- and bronze-leaved varieties within this heading. RHS judges also used to follow this interpretation but have recently not done so, adopting the BEGS insistence on tricolour and bicolour leaves only within this definition.

However, apart from the above minor difference, exhibitors can take heart from the fact that almost certainly a group of good judges, even if each was operating under a different set of 'rules', would ensure that justice prevailed by reaching the same conclusion on the relative merits of the plants set before them. It is worthwhile for exhibitors to establish which 'rules' their exhibits are to be judged under, but it is not of paramount importance, provided proper attention has been given to the commonly accepted meritorious aspects of specimen geranium plants.

CLASSIFICATION

Some interpretations and definitions are required to clarify the above table. We will initially consider the 'classification'. It would obviously be a considerable advantage if one of the recognized bodies could produce a classification list clearly indicating the various characteristics of all varieties within the bands set out in the classification table (page 97). However, while an Australian society have been appointed as the international nomenclature authority for geraniums and are manfully tackling the task, it is awesome in its scope and size, having been virtually ignored, so far as cultivars are concerned, for too long. Exhibitors must therefore decide for themselves whether a particular variety meets the description in the show schedule, but the following may remove some doubts in the minds of beginners.

ORNAMENTAL-LEAVED ZONALS

This grouping includes only zonal varieties having tricoloured leaves, cream and green leaves and white and green leaves.

ORNAMENTAL IVY-LEAVED

This covers all ivy-leaved varieties having white or cream veined leaves or having leaves of two or more distinct colours other than the basic zone.

ZONALS (other than ornamental above) are all basic, dwarf and miniature zonal varieties, whether green or gold/bronze in foliage colour, including 'Stella' varieties. Genetic hybrid ivy-leaved varieties which display few or no ivy-leaved characteristics, such as 'Deacon' varieties, are included in this section.

REGALS include all such regal types whether basic, dwarf or miniature irrespective of foliage colouring. 'Angel' varieties, a term now applied to all 'miniature' regals, are included and, for the purpose of judging, 'uniques' are given points similarly but should *not* be exhibited as regals unless the show schedule specifically includes them (which would be very unusual).

IVY (other than ornamental above) is the term for all basic, dwarf or miniature ivy-leaved varieties. Hybrid ivy-leaved varieties are given points similarly but unless specifically allowed in the schedule wording they should *not* be exhibited as an ivy-leaved variety, although genetic hybrid ivy-leaved varieties showing few or no zonal characteristics are treated as ivy-leaved varieties.

'SCENTED-LEAVED' AND 'SPECIES' includes all species, whether scented or not, and all scented hybrids. The term 'scented' relates to specific scents such as apple, nutmeg, citrus; not to the 'geranium smell' often associated with zonals and ivy-leaved.

While geranium societies' shows generally provide specific classes for the vast majority of different types of plants so that like compete with like, this is seldom possible at smaller local shows or even large well-known shows which have to accommodate the whole range of gardeners' fancies—from Alpines to Zinnias. This should not prevent the best plant from succeeding, however, even in a class for 'One specimen geranium plant' when ivy-leaved, tricolour zonals and scented-leaved types may find themselves in direct competition with basic zonals and regals. Provided the judge knows what he is doing and judges (points) each plant on its own—that is an ivy-leaved as an ivy-leaved, a tricolour as a tricolour and a regal as a regal—then the most meritorious plant should prevail. An experienced judge may not physically allocate points to all, or indeed any, plants in a particular class in order to perform his principal duty of selecting the three best exhibits in their order of merit. His decision will however be justifiable by application of one of the societies' points tables and on no other basis.

We can now consider the various 'qualities' of plants (cut blooms will be discussed later) and the unsatisfactory aspects which result in the loss of points.

CULTURAL QUALITY
This relates to the general shape and appearance of the plant, and reflects not only its image on the day of the show but the work that has gone into the cultivation in the months leading up to the show.

Penalties are Imposed If ...
1. The plant is disproportionate to the size of its pot. A plant grown in the common bush shape would generally be approxi-

mately twice as broad as it is high (excluding flowers) above soil level, and the height should be at least equivalent to the diameter of the pot to give an overall proportionate effect.

2. The plant itself is disproportionate in height or width. Thus a tall narrow plant or a short broad plant would attract penalties, whereas an equally tall plant could avoid penalty if it had filled out sideways, to about twice its height.

3. The plant is misshapen, either as a result of being drawn to one side by the light or because all its major stems have grown to one side, not being adequately stopped or trained to counteract this tendency. The centre of the plant should appear to be directly over the centre of the pot, so that it appears well balanced and uniform from whichever side it is viewed.

4. Bare stems are visible between the rim of the pot and the lower leaves, the penalty varying according to the amount of bare stem to be seen.

5. There is evidence of disease or pests.

6. The plant is lacking in freshness.

7. The plant is unclean—dusty, powdered with insecticide or even with bird droppings.

8. Overall discolouration of foliage is present.

9. Stems or foliage are excessively lush or weak.

10. Flowerheads are too close or too far above the foliage, so giving a displeasing overall effect.

11. Scented-leaved varieties lack scent.

No single adverse feature above should incur a penalty of more than one-third of the total points available for cultural quality. This maximum penalty of one-third of the total available applies to each 'quality' section, other than uniformity and effect when groups or collections are involved.

FOLIAGE
This section applies specifically to the appearance and condition of the leaves of the plant.

Penalties are Imposed For ...
1. Damaged leaves, whether caused by accidental mishandling or pests.

2. Leaves that have grown in a deformed manner—any of these should be removed as soon as they have formed, so that subsequent leaves will grow into any space left.

100

3. Individual leaves that are discoloured or otherwise marked.
4. Sparsity of foliage. This can be caused by poor growing, necessitating excessive removal of leaves for any of the above three reasons, or may merely be because the variety does not produce leaves in sufficient number or size—fortunately there are very few such varieties.
5. Excessive lushness of leaves—normally caused by overfeeding, although some varieties do have a natural tendency to produce very large leaves. If you must grow the latter they invariably look better as second-year plants.
6. Dead or dying leaves. These should always be removed before showing, as should dead or dying stipules.
7. and 8. In the case of tricolour and bicolour varieties, poor, dull or faded colouring and poor definition of colours. Ideally such foliage should appear with bright, clear colours, each colour being clearly defined against the adjoining colour. Many older leaves do tend to fade and lose colour, but unless they are damaged or marked they are generally best left on the plant as the spaces and bare stems created by their removal can cause a greater loss of points than leaving them would do.

A judge would not penalize under this section or the following sections for a fault already penalized under 'cultural quality'.

FLOWERHEADS
This section deals exclusively with the flowers, which should be numerous, well spaced, of good size and shape, uniform in colour, well supported by their stems, with a range of fully expanded and partially expanded heads (made up of well-shaped, fresh pips) as well as buds following.

Penalties are Imposed For ...
1. Disproportionate number and 2, disproportionate size of flowerheads in relation to the size of the plant. While having too few and too small flowerheads are the faults usually covered here, it is not impossible, particularly in the case of miniature and dwarf zonals, for there to be so many flowerheads of such a size that they grow into each other, which would attract penalties.
3. Weak stems. Some varieties, particularly when grown indoors, do have a tendency to produce heads too large for their stems to support; such varieties are best avoided for show

purposes, although continuing with a high nitrogen feed throughout flowering appears to help the stems a little, if not the flowers.

4. Lack of consistency, brightness and/or clearness of colour.

5. Dead florets and 6, Marked or damaged florets—these should always be removed before showing. A good tip is to remove every opened pip (floret) from a prospective show plant ten to twenty days (depending on the type and variety) before the show so that there is no need to poke about and probably damage good florets while disposing of dead ones.

7. Misshapen heads or stems. Some double zonal varieties have a tendency not fully to straighten their earliest flower stems, leaving them semi-crooked and sometimes even split. This can give an unfortunate shape to the flowerhead, although nature is a great compensator and does try to cover up the deformity, the pips ignoring the fact that they should grow sideways and trying to grow upright. Unless the head is really unsightly it is usually better to accept the penalty than remove the flower entirely.

8. Lack of symmetry in the placement of flowerheads. A little attention to the probable position of the flowerheads about four weeks before the show and some astute staking or tying at that time is normally sufficient to avoid penalties here. Very occasionally one of your best plants may have to be abandoned, however, because it stubbornly refuses to develop flowers on one side in time for the show.

9. Lack of freshness—usually due to overwatering, underwatering or a layer of dust.

10. Lack of following buds. This is seldom a problem if you manage to exhibit your plants during their first flush of flowers.

DISPLAY AND STAGING

This section is particular to BEGS, but probably only in being specific—most judges would normally allow for the faults mentioned, in one way or another. If this section serves no other purpose than to remind exhibitors that, however essential they consider they are to a show, the visiting (and usually paying) public are also important and deserve consideration, then it is worthwhile. Briefly it requires exhibitors to present their plants in a proper, clean, tidy and courteous manner.

Penalties are Imposed For ...

1. Dirty pots—a much greater problem when clay pots were commoner, but it is surprising how dirty plastic pots can get and they should always be wiped over with a clean damp cloth before staging.

2. Obtrusive staking. Canes and stakes that are necessary to retain the plant in good shape should always be positioned 'inside' the plant and cut off below the level of the foliage so that they are virtually concealed to casual inspection.

3. Algae or dead matter on compost surface. Removal of this is particularly important when the compost is visible. It is also worthwhile gently raking over the compost surface before a show to give a neat, tidy effect.

4. A poor general effect—difficult to define but one of those things you will always recognise when you see it.

5. Absence of, poor or over-elaborate labelling. Every plant exhibited should be accompanied by a simple white card on which the name of the variety has been neatly and clearly printed. This can either be laid on the staging in front of the exhibit in a prominent position, or fixed to a cane in the pot so that it is displayed above the plant. It should never detract from the plant however, and unsightly scribbled labels can do so as much as elaborately styled printing can.

If the name of the variety is not known the label should state clearly 'Name unknown' (you may find the judge obliges by writing on the name), or if it is a new seedling not yet christened, 'Unnamed seedling' will suffice. You could lose a point for incorrectly naming a variety but judges are unlikely to penalise for this unless they have to separate two otherwise equal exhibits, which very rarely occurs.

UNIFORMITY AND EFFECT

This section applies only when two or more specimen plants are shown together as one exhibit. In such cases each plant is assessed separately, as already discussed, and up to a further 10 points for each plant are then allocated (no penalties, as such, in this instance) for the uniformity of the plants and the overall effect. Thus in a class requiring three specimen plants 30 points would be available in addition to the possible 300 already mentioned.

Uniformity

That's an all-embracing term and while intended principally to apply to the size of the plants, it will also take into account similarity of type, equality of blooms and even use of the same type and size of pots. All the plants entered in such classes should be as alike as possible, provided this is allowed by the schedule wording. Some schedules require, for example, 'three zonals, consisting of one miniature, one dwarf and one basic type'; obviously, uniformity of size is then the last thing wanted by the organisers, but the judge should nevertheless look for uniformity of proportion, shape and number of flowers and pots of the same colour and style.

Most 'group' classes now specify 'distinct varieties', whereas not so long ago the fashion was to produce similar plants of the same variety, which virtually guaranteed a high score for uniformity. In a two-plant 'group', two totally contrasting plants would, of course, be regarded as being non-uniform, but if a further plant, similar to one of the others, was added and entered in a three-plant 'group' only one would be non-uniform. In most cases it is preferable for groups to consist of all single-flowered varieties or all double-flowered varieties, all green-leaved or all tricolour-leaved, all basic types or all miniatures, all regal or all zonal, all species or all ivy-leaved, and so on.

Effect

This is intended to cover the overall impression given by the exhibit, and it is always worthwhile experimenting with plants in different positions within a group. As an obvious example, in a three-pot class where you intend to show two plants with red flowers and one with white, you might well display the white in the middle, flanked by the reds. If the plants were of three different colours, however, they should be tried in different positions within the group, and the group itself could be re-arranged—try three along the staging or three across the staging, two plants behind one or one plant behind two. If it is necessary or preferable to display one or more plants behind another, don't be afraid to raise the rear plant(s) by standing it on a block of wood or upturned pot to gain the best effect.

Very large groups are usually termed collections or displays, and normally consist of a massed effect, rather than individual

104

specimen plants which can be viewed all round. Such collections are not assessed by the previously mentioned standards but for three equally-ranked qualities: overall effect, the apparent (judges would be very reluctant to disturb such an exhibit) cultural quality of the plants and the diversity of varieties.

MINIATURES AND DWARFS

Reverting to plants and the previous comments on their proportion and size, we did not comment on miniature and dwarf plants. The basic principles regarding overall height and width, and the plant needing to be at least as high as the pot and about twice as wide as its diameter, are also applicable to these smaller plants. Exhibition miniature plants should always be grown in a $3\frac{1}{2}$ in pot and dwarfs in a $4\frac{1}{2}$ in pot. Indeed most schedules will specify these as the maximum size allowed. Judges should take into account the size of the leaves, flowerheads and individual florets for such plants, all of which should be noticeably smaller in a miniature than in a dwarf and smaller in a dwarf than in a basic type.

The BEGS attempted to apply three overriding principles when formulating their 'rules'. These were that the requirements asked of a judge should not be too onerous, that the exhibitor should be encouraged, by the removal of any unnecessary and arbitrary restrictions and intricacies, and that as far as possible the judges' decisions should appear reasonable to the general public. To comply with the second and third principles just stated, the BPGS insistence on 5 in (13 cm) and 8 in (20 cm) maximum height for miniature or dwarf plants respectively (one millimetre over would earn disqualification) is omitted from the BEGS rules, although they wholeheartedly endorse the intention of the size limits, including incidentally $3\frac{1}{2}$ in (9 cm) maximum leaf-width for miniatures. It is therefore important to try and grow within these sizes for exhibition purposes and, of course, if the show schedule specifies the BPGS maximum heights, don't risk disqualification with plants slightly larger; BEGS judges will not actually disqualify but they will penalise overlarge plants.

CUT BLOOMS

A class for cut geranium blooms, usually a group of three or a single flowerhead, is often included in a show schedule, and obviously different judging standards must be applied. Actually the various points of cultural quality are considered, so far as they can be applied to the flower only, as are those of 'uniformity and effect' and 'display and staging', the balance of the points being available under the general heading of '**form and colour**'.

Form and Colour

Under this heading penalties are imposed for:

1. Poor shape—the ideal shape is as much like a globe as possible.
2. Lack of size. The main object of a cut bloom is for it to be as large as possible without becoming coarse.
3. Inconsistency of colour. A variety that stays the same colour even as the florets age is always preferable.
4. Dullness of colour.
5. Lack of freshness—it always pays to remove the bloom from its parent plant at the last possible minute to achieve maximum freshness (not always possible but certainly desirable).
6. Marked or damaged florets. Remove them as they occur, not on the morning of the show when they invariably leave a 'hole' in the flowerhead (and you need that like you need a hole in the head).
7. Dead florets—always best removed from below the flower-head.
8. Misplaced florets. Florets occasionally develop with a distorted stem (pedicle) and these should be removed immediately they are spotted as they prevent the natural growth of adjacent florets. Early in the season some varieties produce a 'hen and chicken' effect—some floret stems develop as miniature flower-heads with as many as five florets growing on their own stems from the point where a single floret would normally be. While this can look quite attractive in the garden or greenhouse, it does not enhance a specimen bloom.

Cut blooms are most frequently required to be displayed one bloom to a vase (not a jam-jar please), usually with two leaves, supposedly from the same plant, placed across the neck of the vase and the flower stem inserted centrally between them so that the bloom itself is held just clear of the leaves. Wet sand, Oasis or even loosely packed wet newspapers in the vase are generally sufficient to hold leaves and flowers in position and keep them looking fresh.

106

OTHER JUDGING HABITS

Another welcome difference between BEGS judges and almost every other horticultural judge is that they will not withhold prizes because of some undefined shortfall in overall merit, the effect of which is to frustrate the natural laws of competition by which the competitor achieving the highest number of points is by definition put first, the competitor achieving the closest standard to the winner is placed second, and so on. Indeed to maintain their three overriding principles they had to adopt this attitude and anyone who has seen the friend of a blind exhibitor trying to explain to him why his exhibit has beaten all comers but only been placed second (to what?) will applaud this stand against the establishment.

The exclusion of gold- and bronze-leaved varieties from the 'ornamental' definition within the BEGS rules undoubtedly results from these rules being the most recently introduced, because the hybridists' improvements to this group of plants during the 1960s and 1970s have enabled modern varieties to compete on equal terms with their green-leaved relations.

It can reasonably be assumed that second-year plants will not be penalized as such, but in very close competition the scars remaining from the cut back, even if not outwardly apparent, may invoke a couple of penalty points which could tilt the decision in favour of a younger plant.

The size of a pot will not affect a judge's assessment of a plant that is in proportion to the pot, as a well-proportioned plant in a 5 in pot will be considered the equal of a proportionately larger plant in a larger pot. However, all other things being equal, the old maxim that 'a good big 'un will always beat a good little 'un' must prevail, if only because with more leaves and flowers the big 'un has exposed itself to more penalties, and yet survived. That is not to suggest that a good judge would penalise a plant with two damaged leaves out of a hundred more severely than one damaged leaf on a smaller plant with fifty leaves, but ultimately, when all else has failed, he must be swayed by the extra care and attention that has been given to the larger plant.

When considering plant proportions it must be realized that this does not apply to height or width alone but to a combination of both, so that a plant which achieves the recommended minimum height but has poor width is not half proportionate but completely disproportionate. Indeed, a plant that is neither tall enough nor wide enough may be proportionate in itself, even if disproportionate to its pot, which is why two penalty headings are necessary.

Penalties for plant proportion to pot size are more usually applied to small plants in a large pot and all but the very largest 6 in pot plants would have a good chance of escaping penalty if shown in a 5 in pot. It is, therefore, advisable to underpot a plant if you are not sure it is going to be large enough at the time it is ready for its final pot. The plant can always be moved into a large pot in the last few weeks before a show if it does grow larger than expected.

It is worth mentioning that while flowerheads should be clear of the foliage this does not mean they must be *above* the height of the foliage. This is particularly important in the case of regal and ivy-leaved varieties where a total covering of flowers, including the sides of the plant, would be regarded as a most desirable feature.

Now that we have established the basic principles and finer points that are considered when assessing how good a geranium is, the next chapter will consider how best to avoid some of the faults and achieve a plant to delight the eye of yourself, a visitor or perhaps even a flower-show judge.

8 Growing for Showing

The major difference between showing beautiful geranium plants to your mother-in-law and exhibiting them at your local flower show is that mother-in-laws tend to arrive on unspecified days throughout the year and, if you are a devil for punishment, can even be summoned to view when the plant is at its best. Flower shows invariably arise in the same week each year and that is the day on which your plant should never look better. The visitor to the flower show who is heard to proclaim loudly that he has 'a better plant than that at home' may be a braggart but is not necessarily a liar. The question is really 'Did you do it deliberately for that date and if so would you do it again next year, please?' The previous general information on timing plants for bedding purpose of home and greenhouse decoration is probably sufficient to enable most growers to have a plant right within a couple of weeks of show day and all that is necessary here is to narrow that gap to one week only.

It has already been suggested that over a three-month period (even in Britain) the weather tends to average out sufficiently for plants to make equal growth during the same period each year to within about seven days. Ideally then, to ensure you have a plant just right on a particular day it is necessary to grow three identical plants, one expected to be at its best seven days before the show, one for the show itself and one seven days after the show. If that is too many then the late one can be dropped, as it is easier to keep the earlier ones looking beautiful than it is to hurry up the latecomer.

THE FINAL STOP
The secret of having a particular plant in its first flush of full bloom on a given date lies entirely in knowing the variety and the date of the final stop. Because of the possible variations between varieties the following indications of a suitable date for the final stop must be regarded as approximate, and any

apparent lack of conformity recorded for future use and reference.

Before considering the final stop it is worth pointing out the value of thinking ahead às, once you have selected a particular show, its date virtually dictates every stage of culture from the day you take the cutting. It will be necessary to count back from the date of the final stop (see below) to establish how many stops you can safely get into the full growing period; each stopping date has to be six to eight weeks before the next one. You may have to leave a plant up to ten weeks between stops at some time to enable you to finish up with something to stop on the all-important final stopping date. You also have to work out when the plant is to be moved into its final pot (about six months before the show is usually adequate for it to be sufficiently pot-bound to be eager to flower) and therefore the dates for the intermediate pot(s).

The main factor in establishing the date of the final stop is the type of flower, in that most single-flowered varieties will bloom two to three weeks before double-flowered varieties if stopped on the same date. It therefore follows that if both double- and single-flowered varieties are required for the same show they must have different final stopping dates. The following approximate guide should ensure you have a plant of your choice available on show day.

13 to 14 Weeks Before Show Day
Final stop for all fully double-flowered zonals, such as 'Carole Munroe' and 'Burgenland Girl', and some species, such as '*P. follicifolium*'.

12 to 13 Weeks Before Show Day
Final stop for all semi-double flowered zonals, such as 'Highfield Festival' and 'Ashfield Monarch', and some species, such as '*P. quercifolium*'.

11 to 12 Weeks Before Show Day
Final stop for all double-flowered ivy-leaved plants, such as 'Sugar Baby' and 'Rouletta', some species such as '*P. graveolens*', and some tetraploid single-flowered zonals, such as 'Ashfield Serenade'.

'Freak of Nature', an unusual bicolour-leaved zonal

110

10 to 11 Weeks Before Show Day

Final stop for all other single-flowered zonals, such as 'Katrina' and 'Highfield Appleblossom', single-flowered ivy-leaved, such as 'L'Elegante', most regals such as 'Aztec' and 'Hazel Cherry', and some species such as '*P. radens*'.

Obviously the above timetable can be simplified by treating the first two groups as thirteen weeks and the latter two as eleven weeks, with a reasonable chance of success.

GENERAL PRE-SHOW ROUTINES

In most cases this timetable should mean that flower buds begin to grow clear of the foliage five to six weeks before show date, and two or three weeks before that you should have changed to a high-potash fertilizer. This is the most rewarding and exciting period as the flower buds develop, too slowly it always seems at first, florets begin to open and heads take shape. During this period watering, feeding, turning, ventilating and even more frequent inspection are essential (the odd prayer doesn't do any harm either!).

Watch for unfortunately placed flowerheads and stake or tie them immediately, pull leaves gently down to the pot rim or into any unsightly spaces every day, and remove any dead, dying or marked leaves as soon as they appear. Any bicolour or tricolour plants should be checked to ensure no all-green or all-white leaves have developed. If so they should be removed.

Fourteen days before the show (a couple of days later for single-flowered varieties and many species, and up to six days earlier for many regals) you should remove every open floret from your show plants, taking care not to damage the following buds. This is far easier and quicker than you might think, and is best achieved by pulling each floret stem down and away from the centre of the head—practise on a couple of unimportant flowerheads first. The object of this sadistic operation is to try and ensure there are no dead or dying florets to remove before the show and the newer fresher florets have plenty of room to grow into their right position. Watch for those twisted floret stems now and remove them immediately before they distort those around them.

Once the show day florets begin to develop, it helps a lot if

'Rouletta', a vigorous ivy-leaved plant that has quickly won popularity

113

netting can be placed over doors and windows to prevent bees from leaving their dirty footprints all over your nice clean florets. It is also important that most regals and some other types with red flowers which tend to 'burn' are given a little extra shading to keep them in good condition. If you normally turn your plants once a week, don't leave your show plants a full week facing one way, but a couple of days before the show turn the opposite side to the light.

Should a few of the florets not last the course, despite your precautions, always try and remove them with a pair of tweezers from below the flowerheads. After removing three or four dying florets this way you will appreciate the advantages of your apparent cruelty fourteen days earlier, as it is difficult to remove them without damaging surrounding florets and leaving gaps in the flowerhead.

VARIETIES FOR SHOWING

If it was not apparent from the previous chapter it should be made clear that while some varieties, such as 'Aztec', 'Regina' and 'Sugar Baby', lend themselves to the demands made of a show plant, some others, such as 'Appleblossom Rosebud' and 'Rouletta', need a great deal more work and attention to lick them into shape; yet others, such as 'Granny Hewitt', 'Distinction' and 'Mrs Quilter', are virtually doomed to failure on a show bench, either by the very nature of the characteristics which make them so desirable to grow for non-show purposes or because of the greater show potential of other varieties against which they would have to compete. It is always the plant itself which is to be judged, not the particular variety, so that exhibitors can expect no leniency from judges towards a plant of a variety that is known to be difficult to grow. Equally no harshness will be applied to easily grown varieties, except in the unlikely event of equality of exhibits. Beginners would be well advised to practise the art of showing by growing the 'easy varieties' for the first few years before proving just how clever they have become and growing the second category. The final category we can safely leave to those experts who have become so used to winning that they decide to let everyone get their own back—the exhibitor's equivalent of suicidal tendencies!

The more worthwhile bicolour and tricolour zonal varieties are generally more difficult to grow well but at least they generally compete only among themselves, which makes for interesting competition if not perfect plants. Many of these varieties prefer longer than twelve months to make good show plants and most look brighter and fresher when grown 'hard', that is in an open cold frame or protected outside area, although they will probably have to be brought into the greenhouse for the last two weeks to protect their flowers.

If the show you are contemplating winning (you are not aiming to lose are you?) is early in the season, which normally extends from early June to early September, you would be better concentrating on regals and single-flowered zonals which perform better then than later in the year, whereas the double-flowered zonals are generally at their best in August. One way to overcome these natural tendencies is to start the cuttings for regals and single-flowered zonals at the turn of the year for August shows and grow late-flowering double zonals as sixteen-month plants to show in June.

SPECIMEN CUT BLOOMS

The zonal geranium bloom is, in its own right, a very beautiful flower and individual blooms grown specifically for exhibition purposes can be a joy to behold even if the growing of them appears to be something of a lost art. It must be admitted that modern varieties have not possessed the characteristics most required for the classical specimen bloom, the emphasis now being placed on plant habit rather than flower size. If you intend to grow varieties specifically to provide individual cut blooms it may therefore be necessary to look outside the normal scope of greenhouse geraniums.

When it is considered that we are looking for varieties that will produce blooms of 22 inches in circumference, or 7 inches in diameter, you will realize the size of the task as well as the size of the flower. Not only that but, having reached that size, the bloom must not drop its petals as soon as it is removed from the plant, as some old varieties such as 'Lady Folkestone' tend to do. To get 7 inches in diameter the floret stem must be 3 or more inches long and there should be almost 100 pips in the original bud to give the full head required. The classical cut bloom will be a single-flowered variety with a perfectly round floret, each petal overlapping those on either side. Each floret will need to be 2 in or more in diameter and should open flat, not cupped.

Having located a few suitable varieties, 'Doris Moore', 'Staplegrove Fancy', 'Willingdon Gem', 'Pink Lady Harold' and the most suitable modern introduction 'Derek Moore', we should take cuttings during the first week in February. The cuttings should be eight-week-old side shoots from stock plants specifically prepared for the purpose. As soon as they are rooted they can be potted into $3\frac{1}{2}$ in pots for five to six weeks before moving on to their final 5 in pot. This last potting should coincide with the single-stemmed plant forming its first embryo flower bud and should be carried out before the flower stem is $\frac{1}{4}$ in long. Four or five days earlier may mean the flower fails to develop and four or five days later often produces deformed smaller flowers, sometimes with split stems.

As there is less opportunity for accurate timing by this method it is advisable to grow four or five plants for every flowerhead required; they take minimal room so this is not too inconvenient. Ideally a good single-flowered specimen flowerhead should be opening its first floret three to four weeks before the show date and from that time the bloom should be given heavy shading. As recommended for specimen plants, all open florets should be removed ten to twelve days before the show date so that the subsequent florets, expected to last for the show, can develop unrestricted—watch for those twisted floret stems.

During the full period of growth the plants should be kept well watered and not allowed to dry out. Bottom watering is ideal, as for these plants only it is preferable to water when in doubt, and bottom watering enables frequent checks to be made and the water removed as soon as no more is being taken up by the pot. A steady temperature within 10 degrees of 70°F is ideal once the plant is in its 5 in pot, so that maximum ventilation is required during the hottest part of the day and it must be closed down completely once the temperature has dropped to 68°F (20°C).

Within seven to ten days of final potting the stem should be growing vigorously with large leaves which are essential to such plants. The flower stem will lengthen rapidly and strongly and the plant stem may grow away at an angle. This is not desirable and a cane should be inserted in the pot and the plant stem tied to it, to straighten it out. About this time it should be possible to remove the growing point from between the pair of leaves that have developed above the flower, leaving the plant's energy concentrated on the flowerhead, with any surplus running on to the two leaves above.

The flower stem will develop with the familiar shepherd's-crook shape and the actual head will be seen swelling as the flowerbuds fill out. A week to ten days before you expect the crook to straighten out and the first floret to open, the flower stem should be gently drawn in towards the cane with a length of soft twine placed about halfway up the stem. If the stem is not yet vertical the twine can be drawn a little tighter every two or three days, so that by the time the crook finally straightens the stem is pointing directly upwards to provide the balanced head we require.

When removing the bloom from the plant it is best to cut it near its base, rather than break it away from the plant stem as this can create a sharp jerk and cause petals to fall. As soon as it is removed from the plant the base of the stem should be plunged into water or wet sand, together with any leaves that have been removed for decoration. If the bloom is intended for exhibition purposes it must be transported to the show with great care and not rubbing against or touching another bloom or plant, as the florets can bruise very easily. One suitable method is to fill a large high-sided (5 or 6 in) container with sand and thoroughly soak. The stems of the blooms and leaves can then be pushed well down into the sand which should hold them securely. If you intend to exhibit in bikini-type vases (with the removable base) it can save valuable time if the vases are filled with wet sand and blooms and leaves pushed in as you would wish to display them. The vase can then be pushed into the container of sand and it usually travels quite happily over the longest distances.

This section on specimen cut blooms has been written with a bias towards single-flowered varieties, because their classical form and style are much more attractive than the rather untidy appearance of semi-double and double-flowered varieties when displayed in isolation. However, these semi-double and double flowerheads are frequently successfully exhibited and here many recent introductions are suitable, although they are unlikely to achieve the overall size of a well-grown single flower. The individual florets can be left an extra two to four days and the less fragile more compact flowerheads may last an extra week from the opening of the first floret so they are a safer bet for the busy showman. They can also be transported to shows with greater ease and confidence.

SHOWTIME PROGRAMME

Anyone contemplating exhibiting for the first time would be well advised to practise at the local show and may find the following schedule of some guidance.

The morning before the day of a show you should give all potential show plants a really good watering with fertilizer so that you shouldn't have to water again before they are judged. Later that day you must make your final selection, ensuring that each intended exhibit complies with the schedule wording—no 6 in pots in 5 in pot classes, no single-flowered in double-flowered classes, no green leaves in tricolour classes, and so on.

After giving each plant a good inspection for previously overlooked blemishes (discard any with pests or disease), wiping clean all the pots and lightly raking over the compost surface, you are ready to load up. Most shows offer the alternative of the evening before the show or early on show day to stage your exhibit and you will have already chosen your preference. Whichever it is, make sure you give yourself plenty of time to do the job, have a look round and chat with other exhibitors— as we've said before it's the most enjoyable time at any show.

Transporting the Plants—and Props

Before that, however, you have to overcome the most difficult aspect of any show—loading up and transporting the plants. Plants have been brought to shows in purpose-built box trailers towed behind cars or bicycles, vans with special fittings to carry plants, car boots, wheelbarrows, or even prams complete with incumbent baby. Whatever the vehicle, it should be placed as near to the plants as possible because it is invariably pouring with rain *and* blowing a gale during the time spent loading at home and unloading at the show.

The plant pots should be as firm and secure as possible in the vehicle and supported as far up the side of each pot as is reasonable without risking damage to the foliage. Ideally, given secure support and ample space, the plants should not be touching each other, but sometimes it is safer to gently pack the plants close together provided you can be sure flowers and foliage will

118

not be damaged. Heavy purpose-built boxes with 4 in sides and cross members to hold pots securely are very handy as are individual concrete blocks with central holes to accept the pot, adjustable by use of folded newspapers. The latter are a little heavy if many plants are to be moved. If the plants are closely packed in a suitable box it is advisable to force crumpled news-papers between each pot and its neighbour as it is put into the box, to try and prevent it lurching or falling into the next plant and damaging one or both. Finally, make sure before you slam boot, door or lid that in doing so you are not going to decapitate any of the plants. Remember, the object is to arrive with the flowers still attached to the plant!

Make sure the flowerheads are not shaking and waving about too much. If they are, a few temporary stakes are usually suffi-cient. Make sure you have the show schedule, tweezers, scissors, knife, brush, small watering-can, spare canes, twine or ties, spare pots or blocks of wood of various sizes, a damp cloth, vases (if you are showing cut blooms), plant-name labels (already printed is better, but blanks if you haven't had time), money, cigarettes, matches and your watch. All that remains is to attend to your toilet, kiss the spouse goodbye, clear a space on the mantlepiece for the trophy you are going to win and leave for the show—if you are running late omit the kiss, you can catch up later.

There will be very few exhibitors who have not arrived at a show with a damaged plant at some time or another. Our intrepid beginner should be warned that there is no more dis-couraging happening than opening the car boot to find the best plant has fallen flat on its face and broken a couple of stems; which is why he will have loaded a couple of spare plants. The best advice is either to have a good cry or to hurl the useless plant to the floor and jump on it—after all it will take only another twelve months of painstaking attention and loving care to grow another. Having dried the tears, the Secretary should be located for your exhibitor's cards which should be checked to ensure they correspond with the classes you entered.

Setting up Your Exhibit
Carefully bring in your plants and place them on the show bench within the boundaries of the appropriate class. If you have accepted good advice you will have arrived early and

should have no trouble in picking a suitable spot on the show bench. Remember the first impression the judge gets of your plant is very important, so choose a good central position at the front of the bench and turn your plant around a few times so that its most appealling aspect is facing the judge. If your plant is in with a chance the judge will pick it up and look at its worst side too (don't worry, every plant has one), but the very fact that he is interested in your plant is a good sign.

If you are one of the last to arrive you may have to settle for a position behind other (perhaps bigger) plants which is where the spare pots or blocks of wood can come in handy to raise your plant so that the judge spots it quickly.

Whatever you do, don't assume you can move someone else's exhibit. It is considered the height of bad manners and in any event with your luck you would probably drop it. If there is no room for your plant or you might damage another plant leaning over it, prepare your plant elsewhere so that you know exactly how you want to stage it and then ask for a steward, who will move the other exhibits to make room or lift one exhibit away for a couple of minutes to let you get to the vacant back space.

Getting the plants ready should not take many minutes if you have prepared well at home. Merely remove any temporary stakes, or insert others if the plant has been shaken out of shape by the journey, decide whether it is better to remove any damaged leaves or leave them on (a bare stem could lose you more marks than a single damaged leaf), decide similarly with florets, brush off any pollen dust shaken onto the leaves, give a final wipe to the pot, place your exhibitor's card alongside the pot with your name facing downwards, insert the variety name card on a central stake or display it prominently on the bench—and then stand back and admire the results of your twelve-month endeavour.

Awaiting Results

When you have done that with all your plants, walk around the show soaking up the atmosphere, watch, listen and, if you get the chance, ask a few questions of your fellow exhibitors— start with a word of praise for their plant, tell them you are a beginner and ask your question. Ninety-nine out of every 100 geranium exhibitors will be happy to look at your exhibit and give you genuine advice, to their own detriment even, if you have not done the best by your plant or committed an error. Fifteen minutes before judging have a last look at your exhibits to ensure nothing has befallen them, that all your class and name cards are in position, that a steward hasn't inadvertently turned your plant the wrong way around, and to get some impression of whether you might get a prize card or not.

Now the horrible wait in the tea tent or local hostelry, hopefully with some fellow exhibitors, while the judges deliberate over all the faults you suddenly realise your plants display. Finally they let you back in and nothing remains but to be a modest winner or gallant loser. However, if you don't understand any of the results, do ask your fellow exhibitors or the judges, if they are still around as most good judges will be for an hour or so. Finally, it will be time to collect your exhibits and hopefully a couple of prize cards, and load up again just as carefully as when you came. When you arrive home kiss the spouse, put the clock back on the mantlepiece (well, it was your first show—perhaps next year), carefully unload and return the plants from whence they came, a little water if needed, a last fond look and a good night's rest. For tomorrow you must start the job of doing better next year.

One final warning—don't panic if your plants begin to develop yellow leaves. They haven't caught any dreaded disease; it is just that a change of environment is another cause of this most common of all geranium complaints. If the hall or tent was too hot, too cold or too crowded, or the journey too long, a few older leaves may be sacrificed by the plant to assist its recovery. Indeed, if you have plenty of other plants coming along why not give the plants their reward and bed them out for the rest of the year? Whatever the result they did their best.

9 Growing Geraniums as Standards

A 'standard' geranium is one grown on a single long straight stem before being allowed to branch out and flower. A well-grown standard is little more than the normal bush-type plant grown atop a single stem. Indeed once the stem has achieved its required height the top growth is treated exactly as if it were a bush plant growing directly out of a pot.

Unfortunately, the varieties usually seen grown as standards are those which lend themselves to producing the single stem in double-quick time rather than those that will produce the bushiest top growth. Granted you will need more time and patience to grow the latter, but the final result will be well worth the wait, although it would not be unreasonable for a beginner to grow one of the leggier varieties as a first attempt.

The show requirements of a specimen standard geranium were deliberately omitted from the chapter on exhibiting as they form a more natural part of this chapter, and we should start by considering the accepted merits and defects of such plants. Firstly, however, we must establish the definition of a 'standard', which once again revolves around the term 'proportionate'. BEGS define a standard as 'a plant grown on a straight clear stem, the height of which stem (measured from compost/soil level to the point of the first break/side shoot) should exceed the height of the foliage above (measured from the first break to the highest point of the foliage). That part of the plant above the first break should conform to the proportions indicated for a bush plant as if the first break were the level of the compost/soil A plant grown as a trailing standard would be acceptable, even though the trailing foliage obscures the clear stem, and in such cases the height of the clear stem should be a minimum of twice the diameter of the pot.' The reference to a trailing standard is to accommodate the ivy-leaved varieties which can make very attractive standards; so indeed do most types of geranium, including regals, but not of course some of the species such as '*P. odoratissimum*' and '*P. triste*' which have no stems.

Obviously, depending on the length of the clear stem, there will be short, medium and tall standards, not only as regards their physical height but also their proportionate height. That is to say a basic zonal which normally achieves, say, 12 in in height when grown as a bush plant could be grown on a clear stem three times that height and achieve a full overall height, excluding flowers, of 4 ft, which would be tall by any consideration. A miniature zonal, however, normally growing to less than 5 in, would achieve an overall height of less than 20 in on a stem three times the foliage height; that is undoubtedly a tall miniature zonal, however small when compared with the basic type. Exhibitors will be pleased to know that the 'rules' do indicate suitable proportions—and the sizes even have names: the tallest are known as *full* standards, the middle range as *half* standards and the shortest as *table* standards.

The table standard is required to have a length of clear stem between one and two times the height of the subsequent foliage (measured from the point of the lowest side shoot, *not* the lowest leaf, to the highest leaf). A half standard should have a clear stem length between two and three times the height of its foliage, while a full standard's clear stem should be a minimum of three times the foliage height. Generally speaking, the nearer these three types are to their minimum height the more effective they will look, but for general garden and greenhouse decoration an inch or two either way is unimportant.

The 'rules' are not so clear on the trailing type of standard, but from the information given it might be assumed that a table standard should have a clear stem between two and four times the diameter of the pot, a half standard between four and six times the diameter and a full standard a minimum clear stem length of six times the diameter of the pot.

A little forethought and experience are perhaps even more important when training standards than bush plants, particularly if a specific height is required. It is necessary to estimate the probable height of the foliage head for the variety chosen, which is not difficult as a well-grown standard can produce a head almost as large as a normal bush plant grown directly

123

above the compost. If your chosen variety normally achieves a height of 12 to 15 in, and you have decided on a half standard you should aim for a clear stem length of 30 in ($2\frac{1}{2}$ × 12 in or 2 × 15 in). The same variety grown as a full standard would be between 42 and 45 in ($3\frac{1}{2}$ × 12 in or 3 × 15 in) and a table standard between 15 and 18 in (1 × 15 in or $1\frac{1}{2}$ × 12 in).

The difficulty with standards arises from the fact that the most suitable time to pinch out the growing point of the single stem is when the internodal length is at its shortest, as this produces the most side shoots in the closest proximity, which in turn produce the compact multi-stem framework so necessary for a well-balanced head to your standard. Unfortunately, the internodal length is at its shortest between December and February in the UK, and to stop a standard for the first time during this period does not really give sufficient time to establish the framework of stems required and allow the plant to bloom, until the following August at the earliest. Ideally this initial stop should be made as the single stem begins to grow away rapidly again in early spring—say 1 March in the UK—as the top portion of the stem should then be a succession of short joints between the leaves and a stop at that time, when the plant is raring to go, produces the maximum number of side shoots.

A first stop at that time of year will mean that the following summer will be spent training the head by stopping every six to eight weeks, without letting it flower, until it receives a hard stop in late September. From that point it can be treated as any second-year plant, aiming for flowers from the beginning of the following summer. The alternative, if patience is not your strong point and you are eager to have flowers as early as possible, is to time the date of your cutting so that the required height is achieved at the beginning of September. The stem can then be stopped and the head formed from the stems that develop at that time. A reasonable head will develop for early the following summer, when it can be allowed to flower before it is cut back hard in the latter half of September, and then also treated as a second-year plant.

With the alternative required heights and the plant varieties available, it would be futile to recommend a suitable date for cuttings to be taken, but do assume the head of the standard will require as long to achieve flowering after the first stop as any bush plant would from its first stop. The time a particular variety will take to reach a particular height only experience will tell you, but at least you can give yourself a reasonable start by selecting the longest straight young stem you can find to use as a cutting.

Once the cutting has rooted it can be planted into its first pot, which should be half an inch in diameter bigger than you would normally use for that particular variety. As you can imagine, a standard can become top-heavy and prone to falling over at the slightest excuse. To counteract this it is worthwhile considering growing from the start in John Innes loam-based compost and clay pots, in an attempt to lower the centre of gravity.

As soon as the rooted cutting is growing in its first pot, a thin split 'starter' cane should be inserted as close to the stem as possible. A 12 in cane is sufficient at this time but make sure it is firm in the pot and perpendicular. Throughout the time that the stem and head are being trained, regular normal doses of high-nitrogen fertilizer should be given at every watering. Be careful not to overwater standards: they will not require as much as a normal bush plant until the head begins to form.

The stem should be tied into the cane quite firmly below every leaf joint, but a broad soft tie, such as raffia, is best as it cuts into the stem less. Even so every tie should be removed and repositioned every six weeks or so to prevent restriction of the stem's expansion, and the upper two or three ties even more frequently than this. The principal purpose of tying the stem into the cane is to ensure that it grows straight and perpendicular, and this will require regular attention at the top few inches of the stem; a couple of missed weeks may be all that is needed to develop a kink that cannot be entirely corrected. It is advisable to ensure the stem is positioned directly above the preceding tie, as stems do have a tendency to creep around the 'side' of the cane if allowed to do so; and, of course, a standard should be regularly turned, along with your other plants. Once the stem has adopted a straight perpendicular position the ties are required for general support only and can be reduced to one every 3 in or so.

If regals or ivy-leaved varieties are being trained, the regular tying-in of the leading growth is even more important, as the stems are more brittle than in zonals and attempts to correct a

125

wayward growth can crack or break them. Miniature zonals, too, present a problem as they make so little growth it is difficult to position the ties. But it has to be done as best you can if the finished stem is to be ramrod straight.

As the stem continues to grow, flower buds will form and while some people have advised allowing these to bloom, this must hold back stem growth and also make control of the stem that much more difficult. In all the circumstances it seems preferable to rub off the bud as soon as it appears—apologising to the plant as you do so, of course. Leaves, however, should be allowed to grow and flourish as long as they want to. They will almost certainly achieve much greater size than expected but this is normal. Leaves should be removed only when they clearly indicate they have served their purpose; they will be gone long before the head reaches a flowering condition, so there is no hurry and a leaf that has expired peacefully usually leaves a much tidier scar on the stem than one that has been pulled off before it was ready.

As the stem develops, replace the split cane with a sturdier full round cane and, of course, pot-on steadily to the final pot, which (for most basic types) will be of at least 7 in diameter. The final cane should be longer than the stem by about half the height of the anticipated head to extend the support beyond the most vulnerable breaking point which, on a fully established standard, is immediately below the first side shoot. It is quite likely that for every flower bud that begins to form while the stem is growing upwards, an unwanted side shoot will begin to develop. These too should be removed as soon as they show. This is best done with a sharp knife, taking care not to damage the main stem leaf while doing so.

As the stem approaches the desired height the probable date for the stop should be anticipated. As mentioned, three or four nodes that are close together are ideal, but if the stopping date is expected to be during the summer (up to the end of September in the UK) these last few main-stem leaves should be allowed to develop outside in the garden, which will have the effect of shortening the distance between leaves. (If the right height is achieved outside the summer period the internodal length will probably be short enough anyway.) This is best achieved by sinking the pot to half its depth in a garden border and watching the watering carefully. When planting standards outdoors, always choose a position sheltered from winds and insert an extra cane for additional support. The extra cane is not suitable when planted out in a pot but additional support can usually be temporarily obtained by inserting two further canes through the head of the plant at an angle into the surrounding soil. In the case of a single stem before the head is formed, these two canes can be tied to the cane in the pot, above the stem.

Having reached the desired height the plant can be brought back indoors and the stop made about four nodes above the point at which the first break is desired. With luck, a few side shoots will develop, and these in turn should be stopped as they reach about $2\frac{1}{2}$ in in length or three or four leaf joints; again further side shoots should develop on the original shoots, and these too should be stopped at a similar length. During this period it will almost certainly, unless you are very lucky indeed, be necessary to use twine to pull some of the stems towards each other, so that an evenly spaced, balanced framework for the head is obtained. One further stop, of all growing points at the same time, should be sufficient before the plant is allowed to bloom.

It is usual for a standard to be grown on and flowered for at least two years. To achieve a further year it is advisable to cut back all the flowering stems, knock the plant out of the pot before September and bed it out in the garden until mid-October, by which time many new shoots should have developed. The plant should then be lifted and most of the soil and old compost knocked off before it is repotted for the winter in a 1 in smaller pot; otherwise treat it exactly as any other second-year plant.

As suggested at the beginning of this chapter, it is not worth selecting a variety to grow as a standard just because it will make a long stem quickly. Unfortunately it will not change its habit when the stem is stopped and the head begins to form. The best varieties to grow as standards are those that make the most compact bush plants, with relatively short-stemmed flowers that naturally grow above the foliage (rather than sideways). There is also little doubt that double or semi-double flowered zonal varieties tend to do better than the single-flowered, as the very nature of a standard exposes flowers to greater disturbance, especially when being moved, which can cause single-flowered blooms to shed petals.

While regals have been included in this chapter they must be the most difficult type of geranium to grow as a standard on their own stem, and many varieties are in fact unsuitable. However, some of the modern 'continual flowering' varieties such as 'Pink Bonanza' can be trained to, at least, table-standard height and look very effective.

Among the zonals, 'Regina' is, as usual, an excellent basic-type variety to start with, but there are more compact varieties such as 'Carole Munroe' and 'Ashfield Monarch' which will make more impressive standards, given sufficient time. 'Morval', 'Deacon Lilac Mist' and perhaps 'Fantasie' will be difficult to better among the dwarf varieties, while 'Chieko' and 'Claydon' are miniatures which are not too difficult to handle and look well when established.

The most suitable ivy-leaved varieties are not necessarily the most compact if a trailing/weeping standard is required. Medium nodal-length varieties such as 'Santa Paula' and 'Schneekönigin' ('Snow Queen') are ideally suited for training as a standard. Ivy-leaved standards should always be pruned well back at the end of the flowering period and the trailing stems not left trailing.

It is unnecessary to look any further than 'Crispum Variegatum' among the species and scented as, given a full twelve months to produce its stem, it probably produces the most culturally perfect standard geranium. Any grower interested in producing a column or pillar-shaped plant will undoubtedly find this the most suitable variety. One word of warning—while it is very easy to grow well, it will prove time-consuming throughout its growth, with its close leaf joints, mass of small leaves and tendency to throw an abundance of side shoots.

'Penny', a well known early 'Irene'-type zonal with an attractive, pale-pink bloom. A relatively short growing variety, suitable for outdoor growing where the semi-double florets stand up well to rain *(Garden News)*

A window box gives the best of both worlds, with upright growing zonal plants and trailing ivy-leaved plants combining to produce a magnificent spread of flowers and colour *(Pat Brindley)*

A small hanging half-pot of ivy-leaved geraniums showing the trailing and rambling effect so suitable for this type of container *(Garden News)*

10 Hybridizing

Producing your own seeds and then flowering them can be one of the most enjoyable aspects of geranium growing; once you have embarked on this personal exploration you are unlikely to abandon it while you still grow geraniums.

There are, of course, hybridists and hybridists. A relatively small group throughout the world, mostly enthusiastic amateurs with a knowledge of genetics, are pursuing their own breeding programmes, usually with a specific (possibly unattainable) aim in mind. They look for something new or different, such as a yellow or blue regal flower, a miniature 'Aztec' or a tricolour zonal with the habit of 'Regina'. The trail often leads them back to the species so that they can return by a route different from that followed by the earlier hybridists in the hope that it will open up unexplored possibilities. The detailed intricacies of such work are not for this book, though we should record our gratitude to past and present members of this group for their great achievements so far.

Almost since the end of World War II, hybridists have been at work on another, no less important, aspect of geranium breeding—the F1 hybrid. Their motivation has been commercial—indeed, advances could not have been made so quickly without substantial investment. The aim has been to produce a reliable bedding zonal geranium that can be grown to flowering in a short time and will give consistent results. It appears to the layman that by the end of the 1970s they had succeeded and future developments can surely bring only minor improvements and variations. The possible financial returns from the available worldwide market for F1 hybrid regals, double-flowered zonals and so on could hardly justify continuing the present levels of investment, and further work may fall to the earlier group of hybridists. Those involved in the various F1 projects that have taken us so far also deserve our congratulations. Even if so far their endeavours with single-flowered zonals have perhaps done

131

little for the amateur grower, they have guaranteed the popularity of the bedding geranium for the forseeable future. This might have waned if traditional cultural methods, needing more labour and more fuel, had remained necessary.

The final and by far the largest group of hybridists are those who are satisfied to cross two existing and similar types of geranium in an endeavour to blend the best features of both into a single variety, or conversely to try to suppress the less desirable characteristics of both. The object may be as simple as producing a red-flowered 'Regina' (which incidentally has not proved simple at all), or as difficult as improving the habit and leaf colouring of the existing tricolour zonals. The explanations and advice that follow here are designed to tempt more growers to try their hand at this intriguing, even exciting aspect of geranium culture. Perhaps some will join this last group of hybridists and from among them may emerge a few enthusiasts prepared to acquire the additional knowledge and experience required to enable them to be accepted as members of the first group mentioned.

There is of course a further group who cannot be ignored as they have not infrequently produced a welcome addition to the range of varieties we grow. They are the harvesters and growers of the seeds produced by nature, normally through the wanderings of bees: plants from these seeds are often referred to as B(ee) hybrids—when the grower is honest enough to admit the random intervention of nature and not claim that they are the results of a twenty-year breeding programme! But there is little satisfaction in growing seeds created by nature when it is so simple to achieve the same results yourself. It is too simple, and inexperienced growers are advised not to get carried away. Too few growers are prepared to discard the seedlings before they have flowered—they just *might* include that blue-flowered one we are all waiting for—and this can soon lead to having a greenhouse overrun with seedling geraniums, the vast majority of which are no better than either of their parents and many much worse.

All that is necessary to fertilize a geranium floret is to transfer viable pollen to a receptive stigma, whereupon the stigma will elongate and swell to form the familiar stork's bill within a few days. A single geranium floret cannot fertilize itself, as the stamen (male organ) develops first and the pistil (female) does

132

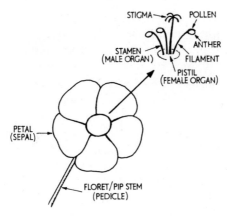

Fig. 4 The floret of a single-flowered zonal

not develop in the centre until the pollen on the stamen is too old to be of any use. This can help you, as you need not waste precious time trying to collect pollen from florets that have developed the pistil beyond and above the stamen. The stamen consists of a stem or filament, on top of which is a small cushion-like head called the anther, and the pollen forms over this anther. Pollen is usually viable within twelve hours of the floret opening and remains so for about twenty-four hours, during which time it is easily harvested on the tip of a small camelhair brush or a wisp of cottonwool fixed to a small cane or match-stick. Once collected, the pollen should be transferred to a receptive pistil. A pistil becomes receptive within twenty-four hours of the five stigma uncurling from its upper point, during which time they are sticky enough to hold any pollen that comes into contact with them. If a hand magnifying glass is used it is quite easy to check not only that pollen has been collected on the brush, but that it has adhered to the stigma.

The seed will form and ripen in about five weeks and should be harvested as soon as the individual seeds come away from the base and the feathery tail begins to unfurl. The seed can be stored but it is preferable to sow as soon as it is harvested, after removing the feathery tail and outer casing around it. From that point it should be grown exactly as described in Chapter 2 on growing from seed, but it is not necessary to go beyond a 4 in pot to establish whether the new variety is going to be worth keeping.

If you have the space it is often helpful to take a cutting as soon as the seedling has made sufficient growth, as the cutting will flower in almost the same time as it would have done if left on the parent plant, and this effective cutback will give you some idea of the potential habit of the parent plant when it forms side shoots. Indeed, if you can wait the extra few weeks to see the flower, which is often no hardship if the seed was planted about August, the seedling should be stopped at about 2 to 3 in to see how it breaks and develops. You should be warned, however, that seedlings are invariably disgustingly healthy and vigorous little fellows and, if stopped, will display a first-year habit superior to anything you are likely to achieve with subsequent cuttings.

The pollen is often more difficult to obtain from double-flowered zonal and ivy-leaved varieties than from their single-flowered relations and regals. If you particularly require pollen from a difficult double it may help to grow one plant in a small pot, underwatered and with little or no fertilizer, which will almost certainly cause it to produce extra and more easily located pollen.

During the period you are actually rushing around with your pollen-laden brush it is helpful if, for a week to ten days before and after, you can protect the plant receiving the pollen from the unwelcome attention of bees and insects, so that you can be reasonably sure the seed has the 'father' you intended. A fine netting completely covering the plants involved is usually sufficient. Attach a label noting the parentage to each flowerhead that you have attempted to fertilize, and of course label the seedling plants in the same way so that if one should develop into a winner you know how you managed it.

If you have been persuaded to have a dabble at hybridizing it will repay you to select the parents with some thought, rather than merely accepting any two plants which between them have available pollen and a receptive set of stigmas. Perhaps the most useful and worthwhile cross for a beginner to try is one between a variety whose flower you favour and another with a superior growing habit—the aim being to breed a plant with a similar flower but improved habit. Most of the resulting seed-lings from such a cross will have something to recommend them and so justify the time you will spend on them. Equally, you must steel yourself to discard most, if not all, of the plants after the first year if they are not a genuine improvement on existing varieties. There are already too many similar varieties available commercially, and if all of us amateur fiddlers insisted on perpetuating our own creations this situation would quickly get out of hand. Once you have decided that a variety does not have enough to recommend its retention it is best bedded out and left for the frosts to kill off, as to give it away to a friend or relative may result in its continuation for many years, with hundreds of unnamed cuttings being circulated, many of which will be given varying names by their owners. If you must give the plant away at least christen it before it leaves and insert a label with the chosen name in the pot.

Even if you think you have raised a worthwhile variety don't become too excited, as the real test will be the plants grown from cuttings the following year. If these plants come up to expectations, then it is time to name it before you allow it to fall into the hands of other growers. When naming plants remember that there are some basic 'rules' which you should try to observe—a maximum of two words in the name, no titles (Mrs, Doctor, Sir, etc), no abbreviations or initials ('Joe Bloggs' not 'J. Bloggs' or 'Bond Street' not 'Bond St'), no definite or indefinite articles ('The', 'A' or 'An') and, probably most important, no duplications. Granted many existing varieties break these 'rules' but pre-1952 varieties are excused, as the International Code was not accepted until then. Subsequent breaches are inexcusable discourtesies to fellow horticulturists, if nothing else.

Now for the bad news. So far we have implied that it is sufficient to take pollen from one geranium to the stigma of another to create a seed, but this is not the case. Certain varieties and types are not compatible, usually because they have a different chromosome count. Every cell in a plant has the same number of chromosomes, but the cells of another geranium may have a different number. Thus some ivy-leaved varieties will interbreed with some zonals, but the chance of a regal being successfully crossed with any zonal is remote. We have previously mentioned that zonals may be 'diploid' or 'tetraploid'—terms referring to the different chromosome counts of each. As a result 'Katrina' (a diploid variety) will not cross with 'Regina' (a tetraploid). Only indirectly is this related to the fact that one is single-flowered and the other double-flowered; for example,

'Ashfield Serenade', a single-flowered tetraploid, will cross with 'Regina' but not with 'Katrina'.

This is too complex a subject to discuss fully here. It is best to assume that if two or three attempts to fertilize one variety with another have been unsuccessful, the varieties are incompatible, and then to move on to an alternative cross. One very rough guide that may save a little time, is that 'tetraploid' zonals tend to have a furry feel and appearance to their leaves, while the 'diploids' are smoother and glossier.

One other source of new varieties is the 'sport' or mutation. This occurs quite frequently among geraniums, with no apparent cause. The regal 'Aztec' has produced several sports, for instance. The best-known is probably the lavender sport of 'Grand Slam'. Incidentally 'Lavender Grand Slam' is allowed to have three words in its name as the Code of Nomenclature requires the naming of sports to relate the new variety to the originating variety. If you should be fortunate enough to have a sport worth perpetuating develop on one of your plants, you should remove all the normal growth from the plant to encourage the growth of the unusual stem and take cuttings from that stem, rubbing out all other shoots as they develop. Some sports are not stable, that is they have a strong tendency to revert to their original form, but by carefully selecting cuttings this tendency can often be eradicated. It is sometimes not possible to know if you have a sport or a reversion. Certain sports are commonplace, such as 'Black Cox', presumably the green-leaved sport of the tricolour zonal 'Henry Cox'.

11 Pests and Diseases

This chapter has been left to the second half of the book because the geranium is by no means a hypochondriac and apart from 'black leg' is almost certainly easier to keep healthy than most other greenhouse plants—so the average grower should not have too much trouble with this aspect, provided a few basic precautions are taken. The rest of this chapter may tend to cause panic, but it must be remembered that most of the problems to be discussed are relatively minor and that there is only a faint possibility that any of them will occur in any one season.

Firstly, however, it must be stressed that hygiene is of paramount importance, and if it is practised at all times, both indoors and in the garden, much of what follows you will not require to know. Equally the very rapid advances, apparently made every year, in the chemical warfare against bugs, beasties, fungi and all things unpleasant can mean that if a particular 'cure-all' is recommended here it could have been withdrawn, improved or superseded even before the book is published. Your local horticultural sundries shop or garden centre can advise you on the current fashionable cure, as will gardening journals and the regular publications of most specialist horticultural societies. Here, therefore, we concentrate on identification of problems, their prevention and the occasional 'old gardener's' cure or proprietary cure that appears to have stood the test of time—but which nevertheless may be replaced tomorrow and become unobtainable.

You may have read somewhere before that geraniums are inconveniently inconsistent, not only between but within the various types, and that applies equally when considering their pests and diseases.

INSECTS AND OTHER PESTS
Aphids
These come in various sizes and colours and survive by sucking

137

the sap from leaves and buds. The greenfly is by far the most common aphid found on geraniums and fortunately is quite easily disposed of once spotted, usually on the underside of leaves. Quarterly watering or spraying with a systemic insecticide is usually sufficient to prevent greenfly troubling you, but should they appear there are numerous direct sprays or nicotine-based fumigators that quickly see them off. They do breed at a phenomenal rate, however, and two further repeated attacks at ten-day intervals should prevent their reappearance. A tablespoon of Jeyes Fluid in a pint of water left standing in an open dish in the greenhouse will generally put off most greenfly (and many humans), as will a couple of pots of marigolds grown among the geraniums—or so the oldtimers inform us.

The presence of greenfly can be a serious matter, as in feeding they can actually inject a virus they have picked up from one plant into any other they might visit; so immediate action is called for once they are identified. If you don't notice the pests themselves they usually advertise their presence by causing unsightly distortions and marks on the young leaves on which they are feeding.

Whitefly
Another sap-sucking pest which, once established, can be much more difficult to eradicate. It will move from plant to plant more freely and is usually discovered when a plant on which it is feeding is disturbed—the tiny ($\frac{1}{8}$ of an inch) flies scatter in all directions. They excrete a sticky liquid on to leaves below those on which they are feeding, which quickly develops an unpleasant mould-like covering. Infested foliage also becomes mottled, but you should have spotted them before that occurs —or you are in for a long battle.

Murphy Systemic Insecticide has proved effective in my experience against both greenfly and whitefly and the regular quarterly watering or spraying is normally adequate prevention, although it is always worth examining closely any new plants introduced to your collection and giving them an individual systemic treatment. If you should suspect a newcomer of being infected it should be isolated and given several repeat treatments before being allowed to cohabit with your other plants.

Once established, a prolonged and repeated attack with malathion and lindane-based insecticides, used alternately every five days for a month, should clear up the problem. Repeated sprays or fumigations are needed because they seldom affect incubating eggs and the flies must be attacked between hatching and laying further eggs.

Red Spider Mite
A minute sucking pest which can virtually defoliate a plant, given the right conditions—hot and dry with low humidity (otherwise ideal for geranium growing). Their presence is usually revealed by the mottled yellowing and drying-up effect they have on leaves. The plant may also appear to stop growing and a slight rust-like deposit (the mites themselves) may just be visible on the underside of infected leaves, sometimes covered by a very fine web.

Murphy Systemic insecticide should also prevent an attack of these mites, but should they occur it can be used as a spray, repeated twice at five-day intervals. Once spotted it will also help if the humidity can be raised by evening spraying, watering pathways in the greenhouse or using capillary matting where available.

Thrips and Other Mites
These occasional visitors are much less frequent than the above sap-sucking pests. All indicate their presence by damaging young leaves, thrips with a great number of pin-holes and mites in a similar manner to the red spider. The prevention and cure is the same as above, with nicotine smoke as a suitable alternative cure and one on which geranium plants appear to thrive.

Mealybug
The largest of the common sap-sucking pests—about $\frac{1}{4}$ in long with a white waxy appearance. It causes similar damage to the greenfly with the same sticky excretion so beloved by ants. Prevention and cure are also similar, with two repeated sprays at ten-day intervals.

Sciarid (Mushroom) Fly
In its adult form this does no apparent damage, but as larvae, small white worms, it eats the plant roots and burrows into the

base of the stem, effectively cutting off sustenance and causing stem rot to develop. The flies are normally visible walking or hopping around the top of compost, and can usually be killed by spraying with malathion or fumigating with nicotine. By the time you realize that the larvae are present the plant is collapsing and it is seldom worth trying to save it. However, to prevent the larvae developing it is best to throw plant and compost on to a bonfire.

Caterpillars

These can be a real pest, particularly on plants in the open, and once the first butterflies or moths have been seen settling on your plants you can expect signs of damage to follow shortly after; eggs on the underside of leaves hatch and the minute caterpillars begin to gnaw away at foliage, stems, stipules and flowers. Outdoor prevention is virtually impossible, but caterpillar washes are available and will considerably reduce the problem. The best solution in the greenhouse remains hand-to-hand combat, preferably carried out around midnight—the only equipment needed being a torch and very heavy boots!

Slugs

They seem to do their best (worst) work at night. The first indication of their arrival are shredded leaves or stems partially eaten through (they never seem to finish anything they start) and that slimy trail they leave. Prevention is invariably a matter of hygiene—plant debris is the usual cause. Cure is to bait the slugs with poison pellets, but do take care if you have children or pets.

Woodlice

They do not cause serious damage but can nevertheless prove annoying and are best driven out by locating their runs and painting these with paraffin. They appear to be another pest which fail to appreciate the innumerable benefits of Jeyes Fluid, so that removal of all debris and rubbish and a generous spray with a Jeyes Fluid solution will soon have them on the retreat.

Bees, Wasps and Flies

No lasting damage is done by these, but they can be a pest by walking all over your beautiful flowers (and scaring or annoying you as they settle on the end of your nose). Nothing can be done outdoors, even if you wanted to, and the rather unsightly seed-heads which they have created by pollination have to be tolerated, although a nearby buddleia, cotoneaster or catmint might distract them to a certain extent. In the greenhouse it is really a matter of having tight-fitting small-mesh netting over all doors and ventilations. A Vapona or similar product is a useful deterrent, as indeed it is for many of the previous insects, but do read the instructions carefully as it is not suitable to work with if you suffer from certain respiratory problems. This type of product can sometimes be obtained in an 'on/off' container which enables you to seal it off when you are working in the greenhouse.

Another method of at least controlling the smaller insects are cards impregnated with eggs of hoverflies at various stages of development which hatch over a period. The hoverflies, like some other small flies and ladybirds, appreciate nothing better for breakfast, lunch and dinner than aphids and the like, so Nature takes its course. Unfortunately this method cannot be used along with a Vapona and the previously mentioned sprays and smokes which are unable to discriminate between friend and foe.

Next Door's Cat
This (or your own cat) can also be a pest should it decide your geranium bed is an ideal waste disposal area. Fortunately, a sprinkling of pepper or one of the specifically prepared commercial sprays is harmless and usually sufficient to force it to attend to its toilet elsewhere.

DISEASES AND OTHER INFECTIONS
Black Leg
The cross that all geranium growers have to bear—being caused by a *Pythium* fungus, possibly *Pythium de baryanum*. It is recognized by brown wet areas at the base of the cutting which very quickly turn coal-black and spread up the stem, turning the leaves yellow. The cutting dies quickly. Black leg does occasionally attack young plants but seldom well-established ones.

Grey Mould
Similar to black leg but is in fact caused by the fungus *Botrytis*

cinerea. It will attack both mature and young plants, usually when humidity is high. The fungus spores are so light they are carried easily from one plant to another by slight draughts, water splashes or clothing. If conditions are suitable they will attack flowerheads, leaves or stems, appearing initially as a damp brown rot but quickly developing a furry grey covering of mould. The fungus spores seem capable of lying dormant until conditions are right when they germinate and spread very rapidly.

Stem Rot
This can be confused with black leg and grey mould but is in fact a bacterium infection, *Xanthomonas pelargonii*. When active it appears as oily grey marks on the stem, quickly turning dark brown, after which the plant will collapse. **Leaf spot** is another manifestation of this infection, sometimes causing leaves to wilt and drop off, but at other times spreading to the stem. The first signs of the leaf infection are damp spots in the leaf quickly enlarging and becoming brown.

Verticillium Wilt
Yet another fungus disease, first carried in the soil, it can originate from many host plants such as dahlias, potatoes and tomatoes. The disease shows itself in many ways, one distinctive symptom being yellowing or yellow spotting of upper leaves, especially where the petiole joins the leaf. An overall stunted dwarf habit is another symptom. Ultimately the stem will begin to rot and the appearance is very similar to stem rot. Unfortunately the initial effects of verticillium leave the plant very susceptible to an attack of *botrytis*, often making it impossible for an amateur to diagnose the real cause of the trouble.

These four diseases are all similar in effect—they invariably kill the plant if the grower does not manage to burn it first. There is certainly no cure, although there are several ways we can contribute to prevention. Firstly, once you have established a worthwhile collection, new plants should not be introduced into the same environment without a very thorough inspection first and, if possible, four weeks in quarantine under close observation to see if any unsatisfactory symptoms become apparent. Whenever convenient, a cutting should be taken from any new plant and the plant and cutting kept together until the cutting has rooted satisfactorily, at which time it is reasonably safe to include them with your collection after another thorough inspection. The risk can be further reduced by purchasing plants from reputable specialist nurseries as their long-term reputation is far more valuable to them than the income from the sale of a few suspect plants. Further, while they cannot guarantee immunity from pests and diseases among their plants, their experience and the availability of excellent government advisory bodies does mean they can take prompt action if any diseases should become apparent, with second opinions on call if they are in doubt.

Once again hygiene is the answer in our own greenhouses and gardens. All dead and dying plant material should be removed at the earliest possible opportunity and burnt or composted. Only use fresh sterilized composts and clean pots and equipment. While it has previously been suggested that sterilizing knife blades is not normally necessary it becomes imperative if you suspect that a plant from which you are taking a cutting may have a disease or virus. Don't give black leg a helping hand with jagged cuts at the base of the stem and ensure there is adequate ventilation around the cutting.

Verticillium in a compost can be eradicated by sterilizing at 200°F but this is a little extreme for most amateurs, and if compost is suspected, it is best spread out under a bonfire and then incorporated in the compost heap. It is simply not worth taking chances with other healthy plants on the half-chance of saving one or two suspect ones.

Virus Diseases
These are many and varied and not uncommon in geraniums, although some may be dormant in many varieties, or at least unable to affect their metabolism, while being ready and waiting to be passed on to more susceptible plants by means of sucking insects or cutting knife. Otherwise healthy plants may show signs of a certain virus only at particular times of year—such as the 'crinkle' virus which is often apparent only around March, when it distorts young leaves after developing yellow and brown spots on older leaves. In good growing conditions the plant may grow out of these abnormalities and present a healthy image, but any cuttings taken will contain the virus and develop the same symptoms themselves early the following

143

year. Worse still, a greenfly may transmit the virus to a nearby but previously unaffected plant.

Another common virus is known as chlorosis, and appears as a yellowing of the leaves, partial yellowing or yellow spots only; yet another results in areas of a leaf being a paler green than the remainder. The only advice for dealing with plants with suspected virus diseases is 'if in doubt, throw them out—and burn them'.

Pelargonium Rust

A relatively modern disease, as far as Britain is concerned, this is caused by the fungus *Puccinia pelargonii zonalis* and appears on the underside of leaves as small spots covered with a brownish rust-like powder which quickly causes yellow spots to appear on the upper surfaces. Spores of this fungus are very fine and are easily dispersed by the slightest air movement, so that early recognition and isolation from other plants is essential; it seems more capable of infecting the other plants around it than any of the previous diseases.

It is not, however, the outright killer that other diseases appear to be and it is often sufficient to remove and burn affected foliage, then spray the remainder of the plant and, ideally, neighbouring plants with Plantvak 75, a copper fungicide or a zineb solution. Unfortunately rust spores can overwinter, so having once found rust among your geraniums you should keep a close watch for its reappearance during the next twelve months.

Rust appears to thrive in cool damp conditions, very like its metallic namesake, so that once spotted you should stop spraying and watering by capillary matting, and even routine watering should be reduced to an absolute minimum; temperatures should be increased if possible. Three weeks of such conditions are usually sufficient to stop or considerably reduce any rapid spread of the disease and will enable you to assess the full extent of the problem. If only a few plants are affected it is probably wiser to burn them entirely rather than risk reintroducing them to other plants after cutting back, as the zineb is an inhibitor rather than a cure.

Leafy Gall (*Corynebacterium fascians*) or Fasciation

A growth at or just below soil level which resembles the structure

144

of a cauliflower head. As the growth breaks through the soil or compost it turns green, but it is pure white below the soil, giving the appearance either of a root that wishes it were a side shoot, or of a side shoot that isn't sure it shouldn't be a root. Such growths start small but can swell to quite a size before you realize that the basal shoot you thought you were going to get doesn't know if it is coming or going. The cause is something of a mystery and the effect has tended to be overstated in the past. If the gall can be broken cleanly away from the base of the stem, the plant—which may have suffered from restricted growth while the gall was present—generally reverts to normal growth with no long-term effects.

Obviously, if you have other plants of the same variety available you should avoid taking cuttings from a plant that has suffered from leafy gall even though there is no evidence that this disease is transmitted to cuttings. Certainly some varieties appear more susceptible than others; it may even be encouraged by restricting the pot size for too long. But it is not a serious problem.

Oedema

This is an enlargement and blistering of the cells of leaves and their stems, which presumably burst and develop a cork-like scar. This is apparently caused by plants taking up more water than they can transpire and invariably occurs in spring and autumn when the weather is cool and damp. Increasing ventilation, reducing watering, removing damaged leaves and stopping the growing points all help to hasten a quick recovery. A more distressing and apparently related form of this condition results in the splitting of main stem, side shoots, petioles and peduncles as if they had been slashed with a knife blade. Removal of the affected leaves and flowers, the withholding of water and warmer drier conditions normally enable the splits in the stems to heal over; rather unsightly scars perhaps, but no apparent adverse effect on subsequent growth.

After growing most types of geraniums for a few years you will come to realize how little the regal varieties are troubled by diseases; occasional attacks of black leg and grey mould perhaps, but generally speaking they are trouble-free. Unfortunately, they tend to be more susceptible to most of the insects and pests, particularly whitefly, but these are manageable.

This chapter includes virtually every unpleasant happening that *might possibly* befall a geranium and the chances of the more serious conditions arising are unlikely. Please do not assume every time an old leaf begins to turn yellow that it has been infected by chlorosis or some similar dreaded disease. If you do, the fun will vanish from your geranium growing and it would have been better never to have picked up this book.

'Henry Cox', undoubtedly the most popular of the tricolour zonal varieties
(*Bernard Alfieri*)

'Grannie Hewitt', a very early double-flowered miniature zonal still grown
extensively. Although of genuine miniature proportions, it prefers a larger pot
than the usual 3½in, so is seldom exhibited. Will produce a mass of scarlet flower
heads (*Garden News*)

A hanging basket of the ivy-leaved 'Sugar Baby'. Because of its dwarf habit it does not trail to any great extent and is best displayed below eye level, where the mass of small, long-lasting, blooms give the greatest pleasure *(Pat Brindley)*

'Grand Slam', probably the regal most grown commercially since its introduction by William Schmidt in 1955. An excellent habit, with large, rosy-red flowers which can cover the plants. It flowers in flushes but is a good exhibition variety when in full bloom *(Garden News)*

12 The Popular Varieties

Lists of geranium varieties can be interminable and it seems most helpful to direct your attention to those that are proving to be most liked by growers during recent years.

The basis for selecting the geranium varieties most popular with reputable amateur growers during the past ten years or so are the combined results of the 'Top Ten' lists published annually by the British & European Geranium Society. As mentioned in the Introduction, each year about fifty members of BEGS, spread through England and Wales (panellists have been difficult to obtain in Scotland and Northern Ireland) but limited to ten in any of the Society's eight regions in order to avoid serious imbalance, are invited to select their top ten favourites from the twenty or more varieties most popular the previous year, and to add to those any new or additional variety they wish. Those new varieties are added to the twenty most popular names on the following year's list to ensure that newer varieties are brought to the attention of all panellists even if only one person believes they warrant top ten status.

Fifteen such lists for different types of geraniums are sent out: regals, ivy-leaved, species/scented and zonals, subdivided under the following twelve headings: dwarf, miniature, double-flowered (greenhouse), single-flowered (greenhouse), double-flowered for cut bloom, single-flowered for cut bloom, bedding varieties, gold-leaved (greenhouse), gold-leaved (bedding), bicolour (greenhouse), tricolour (greenhouse) and bicolour and tricolour (bedding). Each panellist ticks each variety that he grows, has grown or knows well, and from those varieties marks his favourite ten varieties (1 to 10).

When all the lists have been returned, the varieties are pointed, 10 points for a 1st, 9 for a 2nd and so on down to 1 point for a 10th and 0 for an unselected but ticked variety. The actual points are totalled and converted to a percentage of the possible maximum (10 points for every panellist who has ticked a variety—this avoids penalising newer or lesser-known varieties which some panellists may not know). The percentages indicate quite clearly the most popular varieties within each category. Only the top five of some of the less popular categories are published.

One further list is sent to all panellists—the names of the two or three varieties which scored the highest actual points (not percentage) from most of the categories in the previous year's returns. Panellists are asked to mark up this combined list in the same way but on the basis 'If I could grow only ten varieties, which ten from this list would they be?' The combined opinions on this list thus provide a reasonably accurate indication of the ten most popular varieties overall.

Before we look at the results of the lists, it is worth considering the changes that have occurred among popular geraniums since the 1950s. At that time, shortly after the end of World War II, the plant may well have been at one of its lowest points in popularity. This was soon to change however as the earlier 'Irene'-type zonal geraniums began to flood in from the USA; there were around forty-five varieties to choose from by the early 1970s. 'Irene' itself had been raised in the USA about 1940 by Charles Behringer (it is named after his wife), and it gave its name to a strain of zonal geraniums, all double-flowered with magnificent flowerheads in an adequate range of colours (though there were too many reds). The habit was considered compact at that time, the bushy growth and long-flowering period making them much better than most of their predecessors for both pot and garden culture.

In the four years from 1967 to 1970 came three very important developments in zonal-geranium breeding. The first was the release in the USA of the first F1 hybrids, known as the 'Carefree' strain, in eight distinct colours, which were produced by Pan-American Seed Company after almost a decade of breeding work. Many F1 hybrids have appeared since and whether they owe anything in their breeding to the 'Carefree' strain is not certain; but the 'Carefree' were first to achieve popular recognition and they and their followers undoubtedly saved the massed public displays of geraniums we know in the UK.

The second development, as far as the UK was concerned, occurred in 1968 when Ken Gamble of Gamble's Geraniums in

Derbyshire introduced six varieties that subsequently became known, incorrectly as it happens, as the 'Swiss Varieties'. Four of these varieties, 'Burgenland Girl' (Burgenland Maedl), 'Hans Rigler', (Oekonomierat Hans Rigler), 'Countess Mariza' (Graefin Mariza), and a hybrid ivy 'Blue Spring' (Blauer Fruehling), had each won a Gold Medal at Vienna four years previously, but the best of them all—'Regina'— had gone one better and received the Prize of Honour. The sixth variety was a double-flowered purple zonal, 'Karl Hagele' (Gartengestalter Carl Haegele).

The reason for their collective 'Swiss' association was that Ken Gamble discovered them in Switzerland and imported them from there—and very grateful we should be. We might also record the part played by a few enlightened exhibitors, led by Derek Moore of Market Drayton, who immediately recognized the potential of these varieties, plus the 1970 sport 'Pink Countess Mariza', and hastened their general acceptance with some magnificent specimen exhibition plants that thousands of show visitors must have seen.

While 'Regina' was undoubtedly the best of the bunch, 'Burgenland Girl' followed closely behind, while all the others offered improvements on preceding similar varieties. The compact close-jointed plants had excellent foliage and their flowers were as large, profuse and long-lasting as the Irenes, which they and their progeny have now virtually replaced as pot plants. Given the lead he had, Ken Gamble was soon releasing 'Regina' and 'Burgenland Girl' seedlings—six in 1972 alone. One of them, 'Highfield's Cameo', while not reaching the top in its own right was, he says, used extensively by Guy Massheder, of Ashfield Nurseries near York (now sadly no longer trading), in his breeding programme, and it may well figure in the family tree of 'Ashfield Serenade' and 'Ashfield Monarch'. These along with six or seven 'Highfield' varieties, have figured prominently in the popular zonals of the 1970s.

The third development, and the one which may yet prove to be the most important because of their ideal characteristics as house plants, was the introduction of the 'Deacon' strain by Wyck Hill Geraniums in 1970, very appropriately at Chelsea Show. Raised by the Rev S. P. Stringer of Suffolk, apparently from an original cross between an ivy-leaved and a miniature zonal, by 1980 there were twenty-four 'Deacons'; probably no more will be released with this prefix, although there will doubtless be many offspring from different stables. Unfortunately, all twenty-four are not of uniform growing habit, but those which have proved most popular in the 1970s (from among the original eighteen) have been those with the most compact, self-branching habit, such as 'Deacon Lilac Mist'. All the varieties are very floriferous, producing a mass of small flowerheads of close semi-double flowers which are very willing to form real balls of flower. Strangely, Harold Bagust of Wyck Hill Geraniums (also, alas, no longer trading) saw the future of these varieties as large spherical plants covered in their massed blooms, and was still recommending in 1974 that they should be allowed to grow on to 4 ft in height in a 15 in pot. While they would undoubtedly look very impressive grown in that manner, crafty exhibitors quickly spotted the true potential of these beautiful plants—as dwarfs in $4\frac{1}{2}$ in pots, at which size they become just about the best windowsill geraniums you are ever likely to come across.

This is not to suggest that no progress has been made with regals and ivy-leaved varieties in the past thirty years, or for that matter with other types of zonals. The progress in those sections has been steadier and consequently less spectacular—apart perhaps from the arrival of the dwarf ivy-leaved 'Sugar Baby', which unfortunately is sterile and leads us nowhere. Popular regals in particular are very different from their pre-war counterparts, William E. Schmidt of California would probably still be at the fore if he hadn't been misled into believing he was not as young as he used to be and retired. The trend has been towards 'continuous' flowering and a bushy compact habit, with 'Pink Bonanza' (1966) and 'Aztec' (1962) respectively being notable examples from Mr Schmidt of the steady progress made. He recollects his earliest remontant regal seedling as 'Bettina' in 1949, with 'El Elcanto' (1955) and 'Gibson Girl' (1959) improving this characteristic quite slowly —the seventeen years from 1949 to 'Pink Bonanza' in 1966 give some idea of the thoroughness and patience required of leading hybridists. Dennis Fielding of Hazel Grove, near Stockport, has worked almost exclusively in recent years from regals raised by Wm E. Schmidt and has maintained a flow of good ones identified by the 'Hazel' prefix, of which 'Hazel Cherry' has been the most successful.

Messrs Hartsook, Bode, May and Miller in the USA, Coates

and Morf in Australia and Elsner in East Germany have all been responsible for several varieties that have been well received in the UK. Of the British hybridists the most successful have been the late Tom Portas of Leicester, principally with gold-leaved ('Morval') and ivy-leaved varieties, most of which are available through Thorp's Nurseries in Wokingham; Sam Peat of Bristol, also with gold-leaved varieties ('Boudoir') and regals ('Congresbury'), the majority available from Greybridge Geraniums in Evesham; Messrs F. G. Read of Norwich—'the daddy of the dwarfs' ('Dwarf Miriam Basey' and 'Wendy Read'); H. F. Parret of Cobham ('Margery Stimpson'); R. C. Bidwell of Ipswich ('Claydon'); and the Rev S. Stringer again ('Jane Eyre'), all with dwarf and miniature zonals, most of which can be obtained from Mr Bidwell himself at Ipswich and Thorp's. Many other amateurs play their part in maintaining a continuous improvement, one of the best known being Don Storey of Yorkshire ('Buttercup Don'). Between them all, and those who are bound to have been overlooked in such a brief outline, it seems certain that the 1950 to 1980 period will remain an important era in the development of geraniums with little sign of any slackening in pace in the 1980s.

The varieties described in the following sections are listed in order of popularity. They are all favourites, acceptable in any collection and known to grow well for most geranium lovers. No one panellist (including the author) among those who help compile the British & European Geranium Society annual lists would entirely agree with every one of the varieties listed, or the order in which they appear—but the value of the way the lists are compiled is that it compensates for personal preferences.

SPECIES AND SCENTED GERANIUMS

The species were here first so it is appropriate that we should give them pride of place among these special sections; not that many true species have found their way into the annual lists, as the scented-leaved varieties are more popular and interesting to the average grower. Most of these plants have been popular for nearly a century, little breeding work having been done on them. The scented varieties should and invariably do feature strongly in the all too few gardens for the blind, and are ideal for growing in the home as living pot-pourri or deodorisers. They are also grossly underestimated as annual border plants.

153

All are unusual and not at all what the newcomer to geraniums would expect them to be. Most panellists grow only a small number and so it has proved sufficient to restrict the annual lists to the five most popular only. The ten that follow are the only ones that have achieved a place in that list, and the first three mentioned are so clearly the most popular that they have never been out of the top three even though they have occasionally changed places among themselves.

1. 'Mabel Grey' The only recent (1960) introduction in this section and perhaps with the strongest scent of all. Not a strong-growing plant, nor easy to grow, the stems becoming woody more quickly than most. The leaves are rough and deeply serrated with a heavy lemon citrus scent, while the flowers are small, almost insignificant.

2. 'Lady Plymouth' A variegated *P. graveolens*, the green leaves having a thin white margin of varying width; apparently known for well over a hundred years. A strong and vigorous grower, but it can easily be trained to a well-shaped plant by regular stopping and is consequently popular with exhibitors. The leaves have five deep lobes and are plentiful, giving a dense appearance. They are generally described as having a rose scent, but this may be a misleading description to intending purchasers, although it is certainly one of the pleasanter aromas and is popular in the house. The flowers are small and pink with purple markings on the upper two petals.

3. *Fragrans Variegata* A green-and-white variegated form of *P. fragrans* with similar small, downy, heart-shaped (three gently rounded lobes) leaves on a small bushy plant. The flowers are small and white with red veins on the upper two petals only. The scent is difficult to define, being variously described as pine/nutmeg/spicy/lemon and probably therefore having a bit of each. This is a charming little variety that seems to grow well for almost everyone who is prepared to accept the necessary chore of removing the hundreds of small leaves that die off during a normal season. It performs perfectly satisfactorily when grown as a dwarf in a $4\frac{1}{2}$ in pot and, therefore, makes an excellent windowsill plant—absorbing those household smells at the same time.

4. *Crispum Variegatum* Would almost certainly be rated more highly if it grew as well for everyone as it does for some. A green-and-cream variegated form of *P. crispum*, with similar erect habit on remarkably short-jointed stems which are very willing to produce side shoots (whether stopped or not), giving a compact bushy appearance. The leaves are undoubtedly lemon scented, almost round, crisp and crinkly (some say curled). The flowers are small, pale mauve with darker feathering on the upper petals. Not always the easiest of plants to grow and doesn't appreciate British winters, preferring higher temperatures than most. It is another multi-leaved, time-consuming plant that can repay you well especially when trained as a standard. It is well over a hundred years old.

5. 'Prince of Orange' Another centenarian, not as widely grown as many others but well favoured by those who grow it. The plant has an upright habit of very thin stems not too easily trained to a bush shape. The small leaves are dark green, almost round. As the name suggests, it has a distinctive orange scent. Flowers are pale purple with darker veins and of medium size.

6. 'P. echinatum' It is nearly two hundred years since the first recorded introduction of this true specie to Britain. Sometimes referred to as 'the prickly geranium' because of its thorn-like stipules, it is in fact a tuberous-rooted succulent—but a pelargonium for all that. It has a naturally erect habit but can be trained as a bush with patience, although the gently lobed, heart-shaped leaves with their hairy undersides are not profuse. Their velvety dark green colour is attractive, but as the plant is deciduous it is not an all-year-round attraction. The long-stemmed flowers are delightful and there are several hybrid forms varying from *P. echinatum* 'Album' (the sweetheart geranium) with its white flowers and red heart-shaped blotches on the two larger upper petals to *P. echinatum* 'Stapletonii' with mauve flowers and magenta markings.

7. 'Little Gem' Another dwarf grower with that indescribable spicy-sweet scent. The habit is compact and bushy, with a profusion of feathery multi-lobed leaves of dark to mid-green colour. The pale mauve flowers only just clear the foliage but can appear in large numbers making this an excellent exhibition variety if timed correctly. Although naturally of dwarf habit, 'Little Gem' can be grown on over several years until quite large and as it remains fresh and vigorous until later in the year than most others, it justifies inclusion in most greenhouse collections.

8. *P. odoratissimum* A most beautiful apple-scented true species that was first introduced in 1724—how's that for withstanding the test of time? The plant is best grown from its own seed as it develops a succession of leaves from a single crown, only producing its long, thin, ultimately trailing, stems to carry the flowers; these stems do however grow on with flowers, leaves and side shoots so that plantlets can be produced. The flowers themselves are small, insignificant and white, lightly marked red on the upper petals. The leaves are held at the end of long willowy stalks and are almost round, somewhat ruffled with a velvety mid-green appearance. The sweet apple scent is pleasantly strong and is given off in great waves on the slightest disturbance.

9. _P. quercifolium_ Another scented specie but unfortunately not such a pleasant scent—'pungent' is the rather unsatisfactory description normally applied but 'unpleasantly spicy' may be more illuminating. The foliage is sticky to the touch and not encouraging to handle. You will be wondering how such an obnoxious plant comes to be included among the ten most popular in this section. The answer is obvious if you are fortunate enough to see a well-grown plant. It has a shrubby, short-jointed, self-branching habit with truly magnificent dark green, oak-leaf-shaped, glossy leaves with an attractive dark brown marking around the centre vein. The medium-sized clear purple-mauve flowers too are more attractive than most others, with almost black markings on the upper petals of the florets, which are produced very freely. It's a good exhibition and garden variety that has been with us for over two hundred years.

10 'Attar of Roses' Very similar in habit to 'Little Gem', but stronger growing with larger leaves, although still dwarf. The leaves are delicately rose-scented, plentiful, feathery, multi-lobed and mid-green in colour. The flowers are pale purple and appear on short stems just above the foliage.

There are many more that are regular contenders but never quite make the published lists: _P. graveolens_ (sweet orange scent) and _P. tomentosum_ (peppermint) grown for their habit and scent, 'Clorinda' (cedar scent) grown for its flowers and scent, and _P. tetragonum_, _P. gibbosum_ and 'Fillicifolium' for their novelty value.

REGAL GERANIUMS
Regals, or _Pelargonium domesticum_ (_P._ × _domesticum_) as they are

botanically (but much less commonly) known, have also been described as 'decorative', 'show', 'fancy', 'grandiflora' and 'Martha or Lady Washington' pelargoniums at various times and the last two names are still in use in the USA. If the man in the street does think of any plant as a 'pelargonium', it will almost certainly be the regal type.

The probable source of regals is so intricate that it is of little general interest, but it is usually accepted that *P. grandiflorum*, *P. cucullatum* and *P. angulosum* were among the earliest ancestors, with *P. fulgidum*, *P. betulinum*, *P. capitatum* and *P. cordifolium* possibly chipping in a few genes along the way.

The traditional coarse, rather pointed, sawtooth-edged, crisp, dark green leaves of regals have seen some variations in recent times with paler greens, more rounded leaves and even the softer, hairy type of leaf associated with 'Confetti', becoming more frequent. The flowers, however, are what make the regal so admired, with their beautiful range of velvety colour combinations displayed magnificently by large inverted bell-shaped, usually ruffled, florets often over 3 inches in diameter, each head carrying six or more florets to create a dazzling blaze of colour. Many countries have provided hybridists who have contributed to the development of the modern regal, including Germany, USA, Australia and, of course, Britain.

Attempts have been made to subdivide regals into various classifications, but none appear to be simple enough to be generally acceptable and, apart from the dwarf varieties discussed at the end of this section, there is really one principal group—the basic, green-leaved, single-flowered types. A few rather unstable bicolour-leaved varieties have been introduced, without achieving great popularity.

The semi-double classification presents the most contentious area, as many varieties—'Grand Slam' is a good example—usually (but not always) have over five petals, yet somehow the typical appearance of the regal bloom is not greatly changed by this characteristic. Whether such varieties should be classified as singles or semi-doubles is a matter of opinion. At least one genuine double, 'Phyllis Richardson', was released in the early 1970s, but despite considerable publicity it was apparently regarded as little more than a novelty; Greybridge Geraniums were apparently the only nursery still offering this variety in 1980.

They can prove excellent garden plants—lucky growers in California are reputed to have permanent shrubs of regals in their gardens—but regals are usually grown under cover, particularly in Britain, as their blooms are not at their best when rained upon. Regals will generally accept cooler conditions more happily than zonals, not only during the winter, when they continue to make reasonable growth at quite low temperatures, but certainly during their natural flowering period from April to June; exceptionally hot weather noticeably shortens the life of individual florets.

Most of the modern style of regals do not normally require any more than a single stop to create a good bushy shape; further stops should only be used to delay flowering to a particular date. Once the plants have completed their first flush of flowers the best plant of each variety grown should be cut back and stood out in a cold frame, or partially sunk in a garden bed, still in its pot. Within eight to ten weeks sufficiently long new shoots should have developed to provide cuttings for next year's early-flowering plants, provided the pot has been sufficiently watered and fertilized.

The 'king' floret (the central and first to open) of a flowerhead is often not marked as distinctly as the remainder particularly when the plant first begins to bloom—apart from removing it, if it offends, there is nothing that can be done.

The panellists express a far wider divergence of opinion, when selecting their favourite regal varieties, than they do in any other section. Regal enthusiasts naturally justify this by claiming there is an abundance of excellent varieties, to which justice can be done only by publishing a Top Twenty (not Ten)—there's no answer to that. Here are the combined results of the panellists' selections over nine years (1971 to 1979 inclusive). The dates given for each variety are attempts to show the year the plant was raised (the first blooming of the seedling), but where only the date of commercial introduction is known, the temptation to guess has been resisted.

1. 'Aztec' (Wm E. Schmidt: 1962). A plant with an impeccable growing habit, compact and naturally self-branching, quite sturdy and with attractively shaped leaves tending to be a slightly paler green than most regals. The flowers have a white base (flushed pink in certain conditions) with heavy red/maroon markings in the centre of each petal shading to strawberry towards the edge; sometimes the upper two of the five petals tend to have a more intense colour. This is a variety where selection of stock plant is of the utmost importance, as unfortunately the flower can deteriorate from its showy eye-catching best to the point where the floret and markings are small, dull and almost unattractive. At its best, however, the full large flowerheads will initially appear in profusion, virtually to cover the upper foliage; it will continue in flower, but not as profusely, for several months.

2. 'Hazel Cherry' (Dennis Fielding: 1971.) Well named for its charming cherry-red flowers with brown/black feathering on all petals. Another compact, self-branching variety which can usually be left to its own devices to form a bushy well-shaped plant. It is sturdier and has larger, darker green leaves than 'Aztec', but has a similar flowering habit with equally large florets and flowerheads which appreciate shading.

Each of these two varieties has been the most popular regal variety three times in the past six years and when not placed first has been a clear second.

3. 'Country Girl' (Schmidt: 1963.) This one drifted out of the Top Ten after 1976 but was certainly the most popular regal in the six years up to then. Another self-branching variety, but with fewer and softer leaves. The florets are large soft pink with the upper two petals blotched deep red, the lower three being feathered and spotted in the same colour. This variety retains its lower leaves even better than other regals and the flowerheads too will continue to appear well after autumn. It undoubtedly grows better in some localities than in others and wherever it grows it will prove difficult to find a suitable cutting that does not have a flower bud developing—the solution is simply to remove the flower bud and proceed with the cutting in the normal way.

4. 'Lavender Grand Slam' (Schmidt: 1953.) This is a sport from 'Grand Slam' (below), both of which are popular not only with the panellists but with commercial growers too. Mr Schmidt is surprised that this variety is more favoured than 'Grand Slam', as apparently mauve and lavender colours are not too commercially successful in the USA. Despite the varying colour shades and markings that have crept in over the years, this is a beautiful large flower, usually having more than five petals with a distinct darker feathering on all petals. The plant creates large full flowerheads in profusion to provide a total covering of flowers, before it decides it has done enough for the time being and takes a rest to build up strength for another, less impressive, mass of bloom a couple of months later. The plant habit is erect but it can be encouraged into a large well-shaped plant with healthy fresh leaves. When timed correctly the initial mass of bloom makes this an excellent exhibition variety. Received an RHS Award of Merit in 1961, and a First Class Certificate in 1962.

5. 'Pink Bonanza' (Schmidt: 1966). One of the earliest flowering of the regals, and its bright apricot/salmon-pink colouring is a welcome and warming sight in spring. The habit is firmly erect and it requires stopping and training to obtain a well-shaped bush, but the long-lasting glossy deep green leaves create an excellent effect on a well-shaped plant. The upper two petals have small but distinct violet-red feathered markings which, with the white throat, help to produce a beautiful flower. One of the most free-flowering of the 'continuous'-flowering regals and if grown specifically as a winter-flowering plant it can be very rewarding.

6. 'Grand Slam' (Schmidt: 1950.) This was raised from a cross between 'Beverly Fabrethi' and 'Marie Vogel'. Swept to popularity everywhere, it was released and received an RHS Award of Merit and their Sander Medal (in 1956), followed by a First Class Certificate in 1961. The plant is identical in habit to its lavender sport described earlier and indeed the only difference is in the colouring of the large rosy-red florets, shading to mauve in the throat. The upper petals are deeper in colour and all petals have purple markings and feathering.

7. 'Hazel Herald' (Fielding: 1969.) An 'Aztec' × 'Clown' seedling, with the attractive-shaped leaves and excellent self-branching habit of the former, which makes it very difficult to grow a poor plant (unless you should overwater, which this variety most definitely dislikes). The medium-sized flowers are waxy white with an attractive orange-red blotch on every petal; in mid-season the white base colour is so white that any soap-powder manufacturer would be proud to claim credit for having washed it. This variety is an excellent example of those that will produce flowers right down to the pot rim.

8. 'Glensherree' (Ken Fishwick: 1968.) A plant raised by a close friend and virtual neighbour of Dennis Fielding—the name is derived from Glen and Sherree, the family's pet dogs. A 'Country Girl' × 'Sienna' seedling, it will make an excellent plant, being compact and free-branching with long-lasting foliage down to the pot rim. The florets are a soft pink similar to 'Country Girl' but with deeper red markings on all petals. A very long-flowering variety which had considerable success as an exhibition plant in the early 1970s. It did exceptionally well to reach the lists as it was not available commercially for many years, spreading the length of Britain by means of cuttings and plants passed from one fancier to another.

9. 'Sunrise' (Schmidt: originally introduced as 'Rose Dawn' in 1967 but renamed the following year.) A sturdy, strong grower, but the foliage can be rather open and will require stopping to encourage a really bushy shape. The popularity of this variety arises from the really large apricot-orange florets with a white throat; they stand out in whatever company they find themselves. 'Sunrise' can hardly be said to have the longest of flowering periods and repeats poorly, but at its best it more than makes up for these poorer characteristics.

10. 'Wendy Hawley' (Frank Hawley: 1973.) Another variety from a Stockport area hybridist which had to rely on bush telegraph and cuttings and plants passed between enthusiasts to achieve its acceptance. A good compact, self-branching habit with large, long-lasting, deep green leaves that make for an easy-grown plant. With its rapid repeat-flowering tendency, it lends itself to exhibition work. The flowers are large and plentiful and make good heads, the white base colour being heavily marked and feathered on all petals with a deep bluish-purple.

11. 'Hazel Heather' (Fielding: 1974.) A very free-flowering variety with the distinct advantage of performing better than most when planted in the garden. The habit is compact, thin-stemmed, with rather small leaves, and requires stopping to gain the width required of a specimen plant. An early-season flower, and like others with this welcome characteristic it will provide plants in bloom by August from February-struck cuttings. This particular variety has flowers with a lilac base colouring and reddish-purple blotches and featherings on all five petals.

12. 'Confetti' (Harry May: 1962.) This is a truly beautiful regal with a distinct appearance and texture to its foliage. The habit is low and compact, although it is not as free-branching (without stopping) as it is sometimes given credit for. The well-cut leaves are a paler green than most with a softer downy texture, as a result of which they show signs of flagging before other regals, and provide a good early-warning system that water is required. The flowers are a rich lavender-rose with darker markings on each petal; the pronouncedly ruffled appearance of the petals is often exaggerated by the fact that there are usually six of them. This variety is remontant (repeat or continuous flowering) and will bloom early in the year, needing as much as two weeks less than most regals to reach full flower after an identical final stop. In fact, it is a bit of an all-round nonconformist, being difficult to overwinter after cutting back, a bit mean in providing cuttings, losing a lot of leaves once flowering starts and perhaps being sterile as the seed-beaks mutate on the plant. For all that it is a great variety which shown at its best, in its first flush of flower, will take some beating on the show bench.

13. 'Congresbury' (Sam Peat: 1975.) This is yet another variety that has had to make its way in life without the aid of commercial distribution. Its popularity must stem from its excellent growing habit—low, close-jointed, self-branching with a full covering of flowers down to the pot rim; the flowers keep coming over a good period. The flowers are of only medium size, a pale mauve with heavy purple marking. This variety has one desirable characteristic that hybridists must work on—the older leaves that start to yellow come cleanly away from the plant with the gentlest of pulls, which is a real bonus on such a compact dense plant. The full value of this variety may prove to be as a second-year plant but trimmed to shape rather than cut back.

14. 'Purple Emperor' (Geoff Colley: 1976.) Bred by a top exhibitor and so it's not surprising this variety is one of the best for exhibition purposes. It will make a good-sized plant in the 'Grand Slam' mould and produce a mass of large lavender flowers, each petal deeply blotched and feathered in a reddish-purple. A later bloomer than many, but that is a good characteristic for an exhibition variety as the top shows tend to come a little late for regals (and a little early for zonals).

15. 'Hazel Harmony' (Fielding: 1976.) Another good exhibition variety introduced commercially by Thorp's Nurseries (as are most of the 'Hazel' varieties) in 1979. A 'continuous-flowering' type, strong-growing, not too densely leaved but well covered, the leaves attractively cut and with a healthy, clean appearance. The florets are medium to large in size and form good flowerheads; the colouring is a mallow-purple base with pronounced purple-red feathering. It will make a large well-shaped plant with minimal training and is another that performs well in the garden where it grows into a very large plant.

16. 'Vicki Town' (Pearce: c1952.) A compact bushy plant which flowers freely, albeit in flushes. The flowers themselves form large heads of medium-sized florets, the petals all having deep mauve blotches on a lighter mauve base. If you can time it just right to catch the full flower flush, it will give any other variety a run for its money on the show bench.

17. 'Blush Mariquita' (Schmidt: 1968.) A sport from 'Mariquita', a seedling introduced by Mr Schmidt a couple of years earlier and like its forebear a very early flowerer. The plant habit is good but it is well worth stopping to build up a good plant, as once it starts to flower, which it will do continuously for a long period, it tends to forget it is supposed to produce leaves as well. Many of the more remontant varieties do tend to forsake foliage once they begin to flower. The florets themselves are very large, the large red flash on the upper petals and similar-coloured spots on the remainder overlying a blush-white base, giving an appleblossom effect at a distance.

18. 'Hazel Stardust' (Fielding: 1976.) This builds up a good tallish plant with larger, softer leaves than usual with regals. The large blush-white flowers with their red marking are very attractive but perhaps tend to become a little heavy for the longer stems that hold the flowers further above the foliage than most of Dennis Fielding's releases.

The two varieties, (below) are regarded as white-flowered and are selected from four which have each in turn attained Top Ten lists once and, along with 'Destiny', are frequently selected by panellists but never consistently enough to earn a regular place in the published lists. They have, however, achieved more frequent selection than either 'White Champion' or 'White Swan', the other two to reach the Top Ten.

'Mercia Glory' (Fishwick: 1972.) Perhaps the whitest white, having an appealingly waxy appearance on slightly ruffled, long-lasting florets which do occasionally display faint red featherings. The plant habit is short and woody, with deep green, smallish, very crisp (easily damaged) leaves. It has an annoying habit of stubbornly refusing to grow evenly, which is probably the sole reason it is not consistently in the lists, as it certainly flowers and flowers.

'White Chiffon' (May: 1965.) A much easier plant to grow to a good shape. Strong and upright with mid-green leaves of good size and quantity. The flowers are pure white but not as brightly so as those of 'Mercia Glory', although they too seem to last a long time and, considering their colour, are not as susceptible to damping-off as some of the lilacs and reds. A mass bloomer rather than remontant, but a plant to give you good value.

These twenty varieties do indicate that plant habit is as important to growers as flowers, and that a variety is unlikely to become a top favourite on the beauty of its bloom alone—there are too many beautiful flowers not mentioned for any different conclusion to be reached. If the continuing improvement in regals is to be maintained we can expect more unusual and attractive colour combinations and, hopefully, improved continuous-flowering characteristics, while retaining the excellent growth habit that many modern varieties now offer.

Finally, it would be wrong not to mention the obvious debt regal fanciers owe to Wm E. Schmidt, given Dennis Fielding's admission that he is 'only carrying on the good work'. Fourteen of these twenty varieties are known to be either his own raising or directly related to them.

DWARF REGALS OR ANGEL PELARGONIUMS

Often described as miniature regals, this group of plants is currently small in number—too small to justify asking panellists for their favourites—but not really small enough in habit to be classified as anything less than dwarf. Almost certainly *P. crispum* figures somewhere among their ancestors but they form a distinct group and fall naturally enough, for the purposes of classification, under the regal heading.

The term 'angel' which is often applied to this type of geranium probably derives from one of the earliest-known varieties in this classification which was popularly known as 'Angeline'. Mr Langley-Smith was mostly responsible for re-establishing them during the first half of this century, even though 'Angeline'

'Red Express', an F1 hybrid, here planted in the open and showing the floriferous habit of such plants. Vigorous, but compact, with cerise-red flowers, in
1979 it became only the second geranium to receive a fleuroselect bronze
medal *(Garden News)*

'Duke of Buckingham', doing what it does best, displaying all the beauty of a semi-double flowered zonal as a cut bloom *(Garden News)*

'Crispum Variegatum', showing the small, crinkly, green-and-cream leaves that give off a distinct lemon scent when touched. A dwarf habit and, for those with patience, perhaps the ideal variety to train as a standard *(Pat Brindley)*

was one of a group known at least a hundred years before that. 'Catford Belle' was apparently Langley-Smith's first introduction in 1935 and not a great deal of work has been done since, although R. C. Bidwell of Ipswich now offers fourteen varieties, including four of Mr Langley-Smith's.

The plant habit is reasonably bushy (with stopping), and the thin stems and small, rough, dark green, almost round, leaves make good plants but have a tendency to grow away quickly once they begin to produce flowers. The flowers themselves are small, in keeping with the plant, with florets similar to the regal, having five petals of which the upper two, at least, are blotched or feathered. Purple and mauve appear to be the predominant colours.

These plants invariably bloom in flushes and are best cut back, to a point below the first flower on each stem after each flowering, to keep the plant bushy and encourage further flowers. They appear happy in a 4 or $4\frac{1}{2}$ in pot and, given sufficient light, grow well in the home.

UNIQUE GERANIUMS

These plants are a distinct group of geranium hybrids, to which *P. fulgidum* is generally regarded as a common ancestor, although this must be regarded as dubious for some of the varieties that survive today. They were very popular about a hundred years ago and the dozen or so that are around in the 1980s are a mere handful of the selection available at the start of the century. They were, for some reason that is not apparent today, regarded as bedding varieties, but if you should obtain any you would be well advised to grow them as pot plants, when they usually behave very well and create additional interest in any collection.

They are thin-stemmed, tending to be woody, but will make reasonably bushy plants given sufficient stops. The leaves are deeply lobed and usually scented, although the scent is occasionally unattractive (to put it mildly). The flowers can be very attractive, however, not unlike small regal flowers, usually with markings on the upper two of the five petals; one of the better-known varieties, 'Madame Nonin', has markings on all petals. The flowerheads are not large but some do flower profusely in flushes, and with their relatively short flower stems are very pleasing to the eye, particularly during the first flush.

Panellists are not asked to select varieties in this section so we

167

have no check on which are the most popular varieties; 'Madame Nonin' and 'Rollison's Unique' can be very attractive and may whet your appetite to explore further.

IVY-LEAVED GERANIUMS

The annual returns of the panellists indicate that this is the most popular section, with more panellists offering selections than for any other section. Perhaps this is not really surprising, as who could imagine a collection of geraniums that did not include a few ivy-leaved cultivars? It is doubtful whether many enthusiasts would base a collection around them, but most growers obviously consider it worthwhile to avail themselves of the alternatives offered by this beautiful and so different type of geranium.

Ivy-leaved types are generally accepted as hybrids, showing the characteristics of their predominant parent *Pelargonium peltatum*, but there are several suggested alternatives for the other possible parent(s), all of which seem more likely to be correct than the theory that *P. peltatum* did it all by itself, being both mother and father. The botanical name *peltatum* derives from the shield shape of the leaf, in that the leaf stalk joins the underside of the leaf in the centre (as one would hold a shield), so different from other geraniums whose leaf stalk meets the leaf itself at the edge. The more common description 'ivy-leaved' records the remarkable resemblance of the leaves to those of ivy, *Hedera helix*, with their five angular lobes and deep glossy surface. Many varieties display a zone of varying prominence on the leaves which gives a more appealing appearance. In some varieties the leaves also have a pleasant smell which has been likened to many things from cucumbers to crushed Hedera leaves—you can make your own decision but few will find it offensive.

Ivy-leaved varieties in general tend towards thin brittle stems with long internodal lengths which enable them to adopt their characteristic trailing habit. They also create a difficulty in cultivation as stems tend to snap off at the leaf joints when not handled with proper respect. Most plants develop woody stems more rapidly than other types of geranium but these are seldom unsightly, even on older open plants. The trailing habit is widely used to growers' advantage, but it should be realised that the thin stems must not be allowed to develop to a length where the

168

weight of the leaves and flowers is too much for them to hold upright, unless they are trained to a trellis or canes. They are certainly not climbers, having no tendrils or other means of attaching themselves to nearby plants or walls, although they may occasionally climb inside another bush or plant merely by using it as a support.

This type of geranium also has a natural tendency to flower in flushes, as if the plants try so hard to please by covering themselves in bloom, usually from every leaf joint, that they just have to take a rest and recuperate before embarking on another flurry of flowers. Unfortunately, these further flushes seldom appear to be as profuse, perhaps because by then there is more plant to cover.

In the temperate areas of the USA and Mediterranean countries the ivy-leaved geranium is frequently used as a ground-cover plant and perhaps this is its best and most natural use. To obtain the true carpet-like effect, however, the plants need to be left *in situ* for two or three years, and unfortunately British winters preclude that. In the UK they can be grown in hanging baskets, in tubs or troughs, on garden walls or banks and, of course, in pots in the greenhouse or home. Varieties for indoors should be selected from those whose wandering habits can be contained within reasonable limits.

Hanging baskets are good containers, for both greenhouse and garden purposes. While it is quite possible to mix varieties within a single basket, this is another case in which experience is the greatest asset. Actually, a basket of a single variety is probably more effective. Other types of trailing plants, such as lobelia, can of course be incorporated in the basket, but in this unashamedly biased book such practices will be frowned upon! Most baskets, whether 12 or 15 inches in diameter, can be filled easily by selecting the right varieties and inserting four plants, immediately after their last stop. One plant is inserted in the centre of the basket and the other three between the chains. These latter three are an exception to a golden rule, in that once potted into their first pot they should not be turned but should be actively encouraged to grow over one side of their pots so that they are ready to trail, if not already doing so, when planted into the basket.

Ivy-leaved varieties are well suited to troughs, window boxes, garden tubs and ornamental walls. Like hanging baskets all these situations are notorious for drying out much quicker than pots and should be frequently checked, even though ivy-leaved varieties can normally make do with less water than other types of geranium. If baskets, troughs and tubs can be brought into frost-free situations with good light during the winter months, after cutting all stems back to about 6 in, they will reward you well for this kindness the following summer. A worthwhile tip is to stop the plants (and actually cut the centre plant in a basket well back) between flowering flushes, to encourage a dense well-foliated plant(s).

Perhaps the most suitable position for the more vigorous ivy-leaved varieties is planted directly into the ground about two-thirds up a steeply sloping bank, where the stems can be allowed to wander haphazardly across the ground, often rooting at leaf joints. Once the plants have settled in, only drought conditions should necessitate further watering.

When grown in pots, in greenhouse or home, the double-flowered dwarf ivy-leaved varieties are most suitable but even these should be stopped at every opportunity to build up a good plant before allowing them to flower. If more vigorous varieties are attempted it will invariably be necessary to tie the stems to canes or plastic trellis once they begin to flower.

As already described, another rewarding and effective way of growing ivy-leaved varieties is as a trailing standard. The method is exactly as described for zonals, as the stems will trail naturally from a bush-shaped head once the plant is allowed to flower. Twenty inches is usually quite sufficient length for the single stem, even less for the dwarf varieties, and the earliest shoots from the main stem should be kept down to two leaf nodes in length in view of the weight they will ultimately be expected to bear.

These geraniums are regularly ready for stopping sooner than most others, and their tendency to require less water should be noted, particularly during the colder months when an excess of water can quickly bring on oedema. Greenfly and oedema are the most common pest and disease to affect the ivy-leaved varieties, but they are apparently capable of suffering from most others, although fasciation may be an exception.

As you will see from the classification table in Chapter 1, there are currently at least eight different subdivisions amongst ivy-leaved varieties. The basic type is found with both green and bicolour foliage, although many of the so-called bicolours have no more than cream or white veins, probably a harmless and stabilized virus. The green-leaved varieties are available in single-flowered, semi-double and double-flowered, and rosette-flowered forms, while the bicoloured-leaved varieties, although few in number, are available in single and double-flowered. For the purposes of classification the dwarf type of ivy-leaved geraniums include those such as 'Gay Baby' that some may regard as miniature even though they are seldom (if ever) grown in $3\frac{1}{2}$ in pots. There are three flower categories under this type as for the green-leaved type.

The panellists' selections under this section were:

1. 'L'Elegante' Compact habit with variegated (green-white) small leaves and noticeable scent. Single white flowers with deep red to purple featherings, smallish but very prolific in flushes. This is one of the oldest surviving cultivars having gained a First Class RHS trial award as long ago as 1872 and another at Birmingham back in 1866. Principally grown for its attractive foliage, which can be encouraged to develop a good mauve-pink colouring if grown in full light and kept as dry as possible. It does not mix well with other cultivars in baskets but does well on its own and is suitable for all types of containers and situations. It can be grown to show standards.

2. 'Sugar Baby' (Crane: 1964.) Dwarf habit with small mid-green leaves. Double, small, rose-pink flowers with darker markings on upper petals, paling with age but holding much longer than other ivy-leaved cultivars and flowering over longer period. Makes an excellent buttonhole. Originally introduced to Britain in the late 1960s by D. Gamble & Sons as 'Pink Gay Baby', an American import. Subsequently traced to Sugar Hill Nursery in Dalton, Massachusetts, USA, who were unaware of its previous origins but confirmed having named it 'Sugar Baby' in 1964 which is the earliest reference I can trace. Apparently sterile, which is most unfortunate as it has a natural self-branching habit and if well trained will form a small bush, being prostrate rather than trailing. The flowerheads are quite proportionate to the leaves and hold themselves upright above the foliage. Not recommended for outdoor purposes but it makes an excellent greenhouse pot plant and show plant.

3. 'Dresdner dunkle Amethyst' (Wilhelm Elsner: 1962.) Medium habit with dark green leaves. Semi-double rich mauve

171

flowers with deeper markings on the upper two petals; forms an attractive flowerhead. Gained a Gold Medal Award at Dortmund in 1969, and was apparently introduced originally by Pelargonien Fischer of Germany. Achieved Top Ten status in Britain in 1974. Suitable for all containers and situations but difficult as a show plant.

4. 'Lilac Gem' Dwarf habit with dark green zoned leaves which have a strong sweet scent. Has rosette (loose) florets, violet in colour with purple veining on the upper petals. It does not mix well with other cultivars in baskets but is excellent as a greenhouse pot plant and as a show plant. It grows well in all containers and situations outdoors, but tight flowers become unsightly when rained on.

5. 'Rouletta' Has a vigorous trailing habit, and dark green leaves. The single (sometimes semi-double) large white flowers have irregular blood-red borders on each petal—a most striking effect. A sport from 'Mexican Beauty', selected by Wm E. Schmidt, in 1977 it was introduced by Gambles into Britain from Germany, where it had been renamed 'Mexicanerin'. During a visit to Britain in 1978 Mr Schmidt requested that the original name be readopted and most nurseries and growers have gladly complied. A little too vigorous and unruly to make an ideal greenhouse plant, it is suitable for all other containers and situations—a real eye-catcher. This cultivar had such immediate appeal that panellists voted it the top ivy-leaved in its first year in the UK. Whether or not its popularity will stand the test of time, as 'L'Elegante' has done, is by no means certain but its introduction was received with great excitement.

6. 'La France' Large, of trailing habit with mid-green leaves. Semi-double, large rich lavender flowers with maroon feathering on upper petals.

Another long-established favourite dating back to the beginning of the century. Suitable for all containers and situations but difficult to control when grown in a pot in the greenhouse, especially once it has started its first flush of flowers.

The above six varieties have clearly been the most popular varieties during the 1970s with the following four trailing (excuse the pun) some way behind.

7. 'Snowdrift' (USA: 1962.) Medium habit with mid-green leaves. Double white flowers (green at bud stage). Almost certainly the best white flower, but likely to be displaced by 'Schneekönigin' in the 1980s. Suitable for all containers and situations, with the usual difficulties in the greenhouse. Can be a slow grower.

8. 'Ailsa Garland' ('Rotherfield'.) Compact habit with dark green leaves. Double deep pink flowers, darker in centre. Profuse flowers. It can be trained as a reasonably bushy pot plant as well as suiting all other containers and situations, and doing particularly well when planted directly into open ground.

9. 'Galilee' (Lemoine, France: c1880.) Compact habit with mid-green leaves. Double, large, bright rose-pink flowers with silvery reverse—profuse. Probably even older than 'L'Elegante', this cultivar has almost certainly been the best all-round outdoor variety throughout the last century, and with reasonable effort can be grown as a very acceptable greenhouse pot plant.

10. 'Blue Spring' ('Blauer Fruehling') (Polatschek Bros: 1964.) Hybrid ivy, vigorous lax habit, double red-mauve flowers. One of the six 'Swiss' 1968 introductions from Gambles and the winner of a Gold Medal in Vienna in 1964. Although a hybrid ivy it is included here, as panellists are not asked to select that classification as a separate section. The colour description does not do justice to this excitingly different hue; for the purist it is RHS Colour Chart 73a, yet with an almost wax-like overlay. Not an ideal outdoor variety and if grown to any size in the greenhouse it will almost certainly require staking.

The above are the panellists' selections, which cannot be faulted except that as a collection there are no red-flowered cultivars. To correct this two worthwhile additions would be:

'Mexican Beauty' Vigorous, trailing habit with dark green leaves. Semi-double, large, velvety, blood-red flowers—profuse. Like its sport 'Rouletta' it is a little too vigorous for satisfactory pot work but is good in all other containers and situations. Itself a sport of 'Comtesse de Grey', it was introduced by Milton Arndt of New Jersey, USA, in the early 1950s, apparently having originated in Mexico.

'Simon Portas' (Tom Portas: 1976.) Medium habit with dark green leaves. Double, bright plum-red flowers. An introduction by Thorp's Nurseries. A good all-round plant which is naturally free-branching and adapts quite well to pot cultivation.

HYBRID IVY-LEAVED

It is clear that many ivy-leaved varieties have some zonal parentage, just as some zonals have ivy-leaved ancestors. There are varieties of this mixed breeding, however, that do not fall conveniently into either the ivy-leaved or zonal classification, as neither set of characteristics has been sufficiently suppressed; they are obviously mixed-up kids!

They form a definite but small group and yet even so can be subdivided into three different classifications. The largest group is undoubtedly the basic, green-leaved, semi-double or double-flowered section, of which 'Millfield Gem' (Lemoine: 1894) and 'Blue Spring' are the most frequently grown varieties. There are also a few basic, green-leaved, single-flowered varieties and apparently only one basic green-and-white-leaved variety, 'Elsi', which is still occasionally seen, with its crimson double flowers.

Most hybrid ivy-leaved varieties can be trained to trail and, equally, many can be trained as bush plants with the help of a few strategically placed canes. They require no special cultural techniques and should be treated as what they are—something between a zonal and an ivy-leaved variety.

ZONALS

Zonals, or *Pelargonium hortorum* (*P. × hortorum*) are the largest single group of geranium types—they've been the plaything of hybridists for over a hundred years. It is generally suggested that *P. inquinans* and *P. zonale* were the prime antecedents of zonals but, as suggested by Derek Clifford in *Pelargoniums Including the Popular 'Geranium'*, it is at least as probable that *P. frutetorum* and/or *P. scandens* contributed to the zoned characteristics of this section. *P. acetosum* and *P. hybridum* are two others that may have been involved in the crosses which have left us today with one of the most acceptable all-purpose plants we could grow.

Zonal leaves are larger, more circular and softer than those of the regals; they closely resemble *P. inquinans* with its rounded heart-shaped leaf with only the suggestion of lobes, slightly sawtooth-edged, and soft, downy texture. The leaf is usually, but by no means always, zoned with the immediately recognizable horseshoe marking. The flowerheads are held on long rounded stems topped by anything from ten to over a hundred

174

individual florets, which themselves range from five petals (single-flowered) to as many as twenty in the rosebud varieties. The florets are generally almost circular, each petal overlapping its neighbours, although there are several well-known reversions to the more primitive flower form of *P. frutetorum* (and others), with the upper two petals slightly shorter and clear space between all petals, particularly the upper two which protrude like rabbits' ears.

Being the most prolific geranium type the variations and therefore the classifications of zonals are numerous. Not only do they include the full range of growing habits, from miniature (some have sought to impose 'micro-miniature' on an already extensively subdivided section) to basic, but there are green, gold, bicolour and tricolour leaf variations and the full choice of flowers—single, semi-double and double, rosebud and cactus, further to extend the alternatives available.

Basic Green-leaved Double-flowered Zonals

These are almost certainly the most popular group of geraniums for pot cultivation. The term 'double-flowered' is usually accepted as encompassing all semi-double varieties having more than five petals. This classification includes groups of varieties that have gained sufficient prestige in their own right to have been accorded popular 'family' names that transcend the usual specific classification.

The first such break from the usual is inconsistently referred to as either Bruant type or French type, which we are given to understand originated as a single sport on an otherwise 'normal' plant. More than one such sport may have occurred around the same time (early 1870s) in France, but certainly the previous diploid doubles were soon replaced in popularity by these sturdier, thicker-stemmed, rougher-leaved varieties with their rather untidy florets which nevertheless last a long time with almost no tendency to drop petals—this group are all tetraploid (36 chromosome count). Paul Bruant had his own firm in Poitiers and whether this group take their name from Paul Bruant himself or from one of his earliest red doubles named 'Bruant' is not clear. Bruant also appears to have introduced 'Fiat' (another sport), which has given its name to a group of plants presumably directly or indirectly related to it and which itself has a sub-group usually known as the 'Royal Fiats', consisting of a handful of varieties with serrated edges to their petals. The Fiats have a grey tint in their foliage and present a compact habit, most varieties flowering quite well in the winter but being somewhat susceptible to disease and not too tolerant of high temperatures.

Two more recent groups have already been mentioned, the 'Irenes' and those referred to in the UK as 'Swiss' varieties. The latter are not from Switzerland, almost certainly originating in the Burgenland region of Austria. Those that were initially introduced into Britain were but a few of thousands raised by Polatschek Bros in the early 1960s. About ten of them gained awards at the Vienna WIG 1964 exhibition. The beautiful 'Regina' was not named but won the Prize of Honour under a seedling number; it, and presumably most of the others, were sold for distribution by Wulliman in Switzerland, who must have named it before Ken Gamble brought six of them into the UK. It is doubtful whether the 'Swiss' connection will stand correction in the foreseeable future in the UK but perhaps history will more properly record them as Polatschek (or at least Austrian) types.

There are other small family groups, but they are not currently in the popularity lists and can safely be bypassed for our purposes.

The culture of the plants in this classification (and the single-flowered varieties) has been the main basis of earlier chapters; and the bedding uses will be considered on page 194. The panellists are asked to select under this classification specifically for greenhouse performance, but the results might equally apply to the home (given sufficient space) or any other situation giving protection from the elements.

The combined results of the panellists' selections throughout the 1970s have been, in order of popularity:

1. 'Regina' (Polatschek Bros: 1964.) A bushy, short-jointed, self-branching plant. The leaves are mid to dark green, with broad but not prominent zone, medium-to-large sized, soft and downy. A tetraploid. The large flowerhead is held erect above the foliage on medium-length stems. The individual florets are almost double, of good size, and are a beautiful pale apple-blossom pink shading to a soft salmon.

This variety is undoubtedly *the* British geranium of the 1970s, whatever the classification, and as mentioned won the Prize of

Honour at the 1964 Vienna exhibition before being introduced to the UK in 1968 by D. Gamble & Sons ('Gamble's') of Derbyshire. The flowerheads are full of pips which do not drop easily, so that the flowers last long after the following bud has begun to open its florets. One of the easiest plants to grow, it is excellent for exhibition purposes, bedding and cut blooms, making it the perfect all-round zonal. It is not easily susceptible to disease, rewards care and attention magnificently and yet tolerates mistreatment as well as any geranium, although the flowers become less double when it thinks you have forsaken it—but then so will those of any other self-respecting double. A clear winner, by a considerable margin, in each year the panellists have submitted returns, and could remain so for another ten years unless a startling red or orange can dislodge it. Surely another pink couldn't do it?

2. 'Burgenland Girl' ('Burgenland Maedl') (Polatschek Bros: 1964). Another compact, short-jointed, self-branching plant. Medium-sized leaves, mid to dark green in colour with good broad zone and a soft almost hairy texture. A tetraploid. The very double florets of medium red-pink colour make a tight, almost ball-shaped, flowerhead of good size. Long-lasting blooms on a very free-flowering plant give a mass of bloom.

Clearly the next best of the 'Swiss six'. Certainly more double in the floret and perhaps of even denser, more compact habit. Many of us wrongly expected this variety to prove a better parent than 'Regina'. It flowers later than the other five and has the annoying habit of not always straightening the flower stem completely (crooked neck) on its first few flowerheads. The flower stems are so sturdy that this can cause them to crack across the crook and the bloom does not develop fully. An excellent exhibition variety as a plant and cut bloom but a little too double and tight to make a good bedding variety.

3. 'Pink Countess Mariza' (A sport from 'Countess Mariza'.) (Gambles: 1970.) A short-jointed, readily branching habit with mid-green leaves, slightly zoned, large, soft and hairy. A tetraploid. The flowerheads are held on good-length stems and the many full semi-double florets produce a large bloom that lasts well. Described as 'alpine pink' the colour is quite different from that of its stock parent.

It was quite a bonus for Gambles when they were first to

notice the tendency of one of their Swiss introductions to throw a very distinct sport. Strangely, the original stock continues to sport, yet this variety seldom reverts. It is another variety with a tendency to 'crook neck' on early blooms, but it will flower early in the season and beds out well, in addition to making an excellent exhibition plant and providing large cut blooms.

4. 'Countess Mariza' ('Graefin Mariza'.) (Polatschek Bros: 1964.) Identical to its sport, 'Pink Countess Mariza', apart from the colour of its flower which is a soft coral, almost salmony, pink.

The third of the five Swiss zonals introduced to Britain by Gambles in 1968. It has all the characteristics described for its sport and perhaps it is its occasional tendency to repeat that process which results in it being slightly less popular—there is certainly nothing else to separate them.

5. 'Highfield's Festival' (Gambles: 1974.) A short-jointed, self-branching habit with lightly zoned deep green leaves, large, soft and downy. A tetraploid. The semi-double florets are of a pale rose-pink (tending to lavender) with a white eye on the upper two petals, and being large with a good length pedicle make a big ball-shaped head atop an upright medium-length stem.

A 'Regina'-type seedling that has inherited all the best characteristics. It is the only variety to mount a serious challenge to 'Regina', and to have achieved runner-up position the year after its release; this overall position in only half the decade is testimony to its charm. It is probably easier to grow, more floriforous and a better all-round plant than 'Regina', but it lacks that certain something, that eye-appeal. An excellent variety for exhibition, cut bloom and bedding purposes.

6. 'Carole Munroe' (Gambles: 1971.) A compact, bushy, short-jointed, self-branching plant with reasonably zoned mid-green leaves of medium size, soft and hairy. A tetraploid. The very double florets make for a large tight flowerhead on a strong medium-length stem. The lavender-pink colour is a delight.

Named after the daughter of Mrs Iris Munro (presumably the last 'e' in the variety name was an original error that, annoyingly, must be for ever perpetuated) of Inverness, one of Britain's best-known amateur exhibitors in the 1970s. Her displays included Chelsea Flower Show—all the way from Inverness.

While Ken Gamble assures us this is a 'Regina' seedling, we must suspect that 'Burgenland Girl' has contributed in some way, as this variety is very similar in habit to the latter, including the occasional crooked neck, unfortunately. The flowerhead is a little too tight to make an ideal bedder but is an excellent exhibition and cut-bloom variety that makes a perfect partner for 'Burgenland Girl' when they are shown together.

7. 'Ashfield Monarch' (Guy Massheder: 1975.) A very short-jointed, self-branching, bushy variety with narrow-zoned, dark green leaves of medium size. A tetraploid. Crimson-red (who said 'at last'?) with silvery reverse; the full semi-double florets make up a large bright flowerhead on a short-to-medium flower stem. Very free-flowering.

Guy Massheder was perhaps the first in the UK to realize the commercial potential of dwarf zonal geraniums and his excellent display stands of them at numerous shows did much to raise the standard of geranium displays without ever gaining their just rewards. His Ashfield Nurseries at Dunnington, York, always guaranteed a warm hospitable welcome. His retirement from geraniums in 1975 was the more regrettable because the breeding programme he had started a few years previously was beginning to show real results. This particular variety is second only to 'Regina' in the early 1980s, yet while it was officially released in Guy's last year of trading, sadly it was in short supply; the few of us lucky enough to obtain one were kept busy passing on cuttings. Without commercial distribution it has done well to achieve this position. Fortunately, Greybridge Geraniums are now distributing the more popular 'Ashfield' varieties and Thorp's Geraniums are intending to do so. The plant itself is low-growing, appears to have a high resistance to disease, propagates easily and is a surprisingly good bedder, as well as being ideal for exhibition and cut-bloom purposes.

8. 'Highfield's Melody' (Gambles: 1972.) A relatively short-jointed, branching variety that will produce a good bushy plant. The leaves are large and soft, a mid-green colour with moderate zone. A tetraploid. The flowerheads are of good size held upright on medium-to-long stems, the large almost double florets are plentiful and coral-red in colour. Free-flowering.

Yet another 'Swiss' seedling from Ken Gamble looking as though it has more than a little of the 'Marizas' in its make-up; and like them it welcomes a little human intervention to assist

179

in producing a well-shaped show plant. It makes an excellent second-year plant and even older stock plants will provide a magnificent show if given a large enough pot.

9. 'Highfield's Sugar Candy' (Gambles: 1971.) A really compact, short-jointed, self-branching variety with slightly zoned, dark-green, medium-sized leaves. The short-to-medium flower stems hold the blooms clear of the foliage, but close enough for the double, oyster-coloured florets to contrast well with the dark green foliage.

The nearest to a white flower you will find in this section and it has never been apparent whether it is popular because of its undoubted natural beauty or because it is the 'white' with the best growing habit. If it is the latter we may find that a new release by Thorp's Nurseries, 'Beryl Gibbons' (John Gibbons, 1978), displaces it over the next few years. That would be a pity as although the oyster colour fades to pale pink as the floret ages, the overall effect is charming and the plant has an excellent natural growing habit.

10. 'Springtime' (USA: c1962.) A compact, short-jointed 'Irene'-type variety, strong growing with the typically soft, hairy, mid-green foliage of its type. Soft salmon-pink, untidy, semi-double florets in profusion on a large flowerhead held erect on medium-length stem. Very free-flowering.

It is only proper that one of the Irene type should have qualified for a position in the 1970s' Top Tens and this variety demonstrates the improvement that breeders brought about in this group during the late 1950s and early 1960s. Willing to produce flowers at every node, 'Springtime' represents almost everything that is good in Irenes and whether it is a true Irene or an Irene hybrid is unimportant to the grower. Good for greenhouse and bedding purposes as the flowers shatter less than in most Irenes.

11. 'Treasure Chest' (Fred Bode: 1965.) Another compact, short-jointed Irene with dark green, faintly zoned leaves. The medium-length, strong flower stems easily hold the large, round blooms made up of large semi-double florets. The scarlet over-laid orange colouring is most attractive.

An excellent bedding variety, considering how double it is, as well as doing itself justice in pots and as a cut bloom. It is a slower grower than almost every other Irene, which together with its unusual colouring doubtless accounts for its popularity.

12. 'Highfield's Attracta' (Gambles: 1971.) A bushy, short-jointed, self-branching plant. Its large, mid-green leaves are faintly zoned, soft and downy. A tetraploid. The large flower-heads are held upright on sturdy, medium-to-long flower stems and the large florets have an unusual petal colouring of white overlaid with a salmon-pink in the centre and at the edge, giving a picotee effect.

Along with 'Carole Munroe' and 'Highfield's Sugar Candy', this is the third of the first six 'Swiss' seedlings released by Gambles in 1971 to achieve general acclaim. Although quite distinct from 'Regina' it probably suffered by being a closer colour match than the others. Excellent for pot and cut-bloom work, but it has never figured prominently in the panellists' bedding lists.

13. 'Hans Rigler' ('Oekonomierat Hans Rigler'.) (Polatschek Bros: 1964.) An upright, relatively short-jointed variety. Dark green, zoned leaves with a softish, hairy texture. The bright-red full semi-double florets have a good shape and form a medium-size flowerhead on medium-to-long flower stems. Free-flowering.

The last of the 'Swiss' to gain mention (the sixth variety 'Karl Hagele' was perhaps too dark a purple to become universally popular). It requires training more than those fellow immigrants already mentioned in this section, but nevertheless it will make a bushy plant and the abundance of flowers repays delaying them a little. Dropped out of the Top Ten after 1974.

14. 'Sylvia Marie' (Gambles: 1974.) A short-jointed, self-branching variety making a good bushy plant. The leaves are mid-green, zoned, soft and downy. A tetraploid. Strong, medium-to-long flower stems carry the large ball-shaped blooms made up of large and semi-double florets, salmon-orange in colour with a silvery reverse to the petals.

A typically good 'Swiss' type, and a real colour break on good-size florets that make an attractive flowerhead. Strangely it took longer to establish its popularity than expected, not gaining a Top Ten place until 1978, rising to fifth in 1979, the last year we are considering. It should easily hold this position for a few years unless a deeper orange is forthcoming. Suitable for greenhouse and bedding.

15. 'Highfield's Flair' (Gambles: 1975.) A compact, short-jointed plant with dark green slightly zoned leaves of medium size. Produces a good-sized flowerhead on a strong medium-length stem. The florets are double, large and numerous in a clear scarlet colour.

This was the last double-flowered variety released by Gambles in the 1970s and completed an excellent range of colours. This variety appreciates stopping to build up a bushy shape and may not be able to overcome 'Ashfield Monarch' as the top red for this reason, as well as its lighter red colouring. A good exhibiton variety for all that, and as most collections warrant at least two reds, its popularity should continue.

There they are in all their glory, the current top double-flowered zonals. If the description of the plants' habits tended to be monotonous this merely indicates the qualities that modern geranium enthusiasts appreciate. Almost certainly all these varieties are tetraploid but such reference has been omitted where I have no personal confirmation of a variety's breeding compatibility with other known tetraploids. Once again, as with the regals, the habit has proved to be at least as important as the flower, and almost certainly this trend will continue.

Having paid tribute to Wm Schmidt in the regal section, we can hardly close this section without paying similar tribute to Ken Gamble for the pleasure he has so obviously provided to zonal growers. With seven varieties of his own breeding, one sport and four 'Swiss' introductions, he didn't give anyone else much of a look-in.

Double-flowered Zonals For Cut Blooms

This is not a separate classification, but a section on which the BEGS panellists are asked to pontificate separately because the quality of an individual flowerhead (bloom) is not in any way dependent on the growing habit of a particular variety. Only the top five varieties are published each year. They have been remarkably consistent throughout the 1970s so that only seven varieties require honourable mention and most of those have been described already.

1. 'Regina'—see page 176.

2. 'Duke of Buckingham' (reintroduced by Henry & Gladys Weller: 1964.) A strong-growing, medium-to-long-jointed plant with dark green zoned leaves sometimes very large. The long straight flower stems support a large head of well-formed semi-double florets in an eye-catching orange-scarlet colour. The

182

'Distinction', a zonal whose dark-green leaves have a narrow, black zone close to their edges, which sometimes results in it being listed among ornamental varieties in catalogues. The red flowers are attractive, but primitive in form *(Garden News)*

'Attraction', a good example of a double cactus-flowered zonal, clearly showing the quilled and furled petals that make up each floret *(Garden News)*

flowers are long-lasting, having many florets with long pedicles.

Almost certainly an old Bruant-type variety renamed. It was discovered growing, under this name, in a garden in Belmont by Gladys and Henry Weller during 1962—they obtained stock and were responsible for its distribution under the new name. To complete the story, the owner of all the original stock lost the lot in the hard winter of 1962-3 so it had been spotted just in time. Mr Weller himself believes the probable original name is the German 'Schöne aus dem Murgtal' (Harteweck of Gaggenau, c1937).

3. 'Burgenland Girl'—see page 177.

4. 'Highfield's Festival'—see page 178.

5. 'Ashfield Monarch'—see page 179.

6. 'Pink Countess Mariza'—see page 177.

7. 'Gallant' (Holmes Miller: 1948.) A strong-growing, medium-to-long-jointed plant with sturdy stems and large, mid-green zoned leaves. The flowers are a geranium-lake red, semi-double florets with good length pedicles building up to a good sized, ball-shaped flowerhead on a sturdy stem.

For lasting in-house flower arrangements the blooms of these varieties should be cut as soon as they have about ten open florets; then they will give a good, long-lasting display.

For short-term exhibition purposes the bloom should ideally be shown about four days before the last floret would have opened, which will probably mean removing about a third of the potential florets as they open, up to twelve days before the show, as described in Chapter 8. 'Burgenland Girl' and 'Pink Countess Mariza' can upset your best-laid plans if they develop one of their infamous crook necks. It is best, with these varieties, to allow the plant one bloom before the bloom you require for showing which does seem to reduce the chances of this occurring.

Basic Green-leaved, Rosebud-flowered Zonals

This classification sometimes referred to as 'Noisette', contains very few varieties and although the perfectionist may demand some guidance as to when a very full double floret becomes a 'rosebud', or vice-versa; the answer here must be 'no comment'. The only difference between this classification and the preceding one is that on the 'rosebuds' the individual florets are so double that they never open fully. A few outer petals will curl

185

back at their tip but the remainder stay tightly packed and look like a very miniature cabbage or rosebud. All the plants themselves are sparse, thin-stemmed upright growers (but not all strongly so), and require hard work, with regular stopping and tying, to achieve a reasonably bushy habit.

These plants were known before 1870 and since that time their numbers have almost certainly reduced, as stock has been discarded. We cannot now be sure that their current names are the original ones and have to take them as they now are. There are probably less than half a dozen still available: 'Red Rambler', 'Scarlet Rambler', 'Plum Rambler', 'Le Febre' and the best-known and most widely sought after, 'Appleblossom Rosebud'. The latter variety has charming white flowers with a touch of green, tinted carmine at the tip of each petal. It is probably the strongest grower and will produce a good standard plant, if time is spent training the head to shape.

Basic Green-leaved Single-flowered Zonals

Until the late 1960s the popular varieties were invariably diploid (chromosome count of 18), and were grown mostly for the beauty of the large flowerheads and/or their excellent long-flowering bedding qualities. Throughout the 1970s, however, the geranium became more universally accepted as an exhibition show plant and the actual habit of the plant became more important. This is perhaps right, but it is to be hoped that if it brings any loss of the impressive size and beauty of the magnificent blooms this will be a very temporary state—otherwise the price may not be worth paying.

The only requirement of a single-flowered variety is that it should have five petals to each floret. It is desirable that each petal should be equal in size and overlie its neighbour sufficiently to enable the five petals to form an almost perfect circular disc—desirable but not essential. There has been little attempt to subdivide this classification, presumably because most breeding lines progressed similarly or became merged, so that no distinct characteristic of any particular strain prevailed long enough to warrant specific classification. However, a few individual flower characteristics have assumed popular names. The oldest of these is the aptly named 'Cyclops', a classification suggested by Bruant for those varieties which display the large white eye in the centre or upper portion of each floret. This is still referred

186

to as the 'Painted Lady' group (after an early variety of that name) in the USA, but it requires some definition as to how big the eye can or should be, whether veining is permitted, whether picotee-edged flowers are included, and so on. It is of little consequence, however, as a very large number of varieties would become eligible if the wider alternatives were adopted. 'Bird's Egg' is another term you may come across when some flowers are described. It refers to speckled markings on the florets—'Rose-pink Bird's Egg'; being a good example. There is at least one double-flowered 'Bird's Egg' variety, though whether any of these is now available in the UK is doubtful.

'Fimbriated, or serrated, or carnation flowers'—the petal edges having saw-like teeth, similar to those on the semi-double 'Royal Fiats' mentioned previously—are also found on a few varieties. 'Skelly's Pride' is undoubtedly the best-known single. 'New Life' is a small group of about four varieties (one double-flowered) with stripes or narrow flecks on the petals. But none of these need concern us. If any subdivision of the group is necessary it would be better to divide into 'single-coloured or self-coloured varieties' and 'all others'.

The following fifteen varieties were selected by the panellists as the single-flowered basic green-leaved zonal most popular for greenhouse cultivation.

1. 'Kathleen Gamble' (Gambles: 1966.) A medium-jointed plant with prominent broad zone on large dark green leaves. The long flower stems hold the large blooms upright above the foliage. The numerous florets are large in a pleasing rich salmon-pink colour, deepening in tone at the centre.

A real beauty (just like Ken Gamble's daughter after whom it was named). The variety has been a winner since it was first introduced, its foliage vying with the flowers to catch your eye. The blooms themselves are long-lasting and the florets do not drop their petals too readily.

2. 'Topper' (Fred Thrush: 1969). A short-to-medium-jointed plant with stems of average thickness and medium-sized leaves, mid-green in colour and with a good distinct zone. The flower-heads do not become over-large but are a good size with well-shaped florets, rose-pink tending to lavender with a small white eye. Free-flowering.

Originally introduced by George Wallwin of Grove, Notts, as were most of Mr Thrush's new varieties at that time, this variety was a winner from the time of its release until it was edged out of the Top Ten in 1977. A good pot variety almost too willing to bloom: it requires holding back by stopping, to build up a good plant.

3. 'Carmine Flush' A short-jointed, easily trained plant with good, medium-sized, lightly zoned, mid-green foliage. Although each flowerhead attains a good overall size and shape, it is a little sparse on pips. The florets are carmine-red with a white eye over all the petals, which produce a full round disc. Floriferous.

Something of a mystery this variety, and probably the author's only claim to fame. Purchased as a single plant from the greenhouses at Trentham Gardens in 1963, no trace has been found of any listing and although sufficiently attractive for cuttings to be much in demand, it has not appeared in the Top Ten since 1975. It may well no longer exist, so don't spend time searching for it.

4. 'Highfield's Pride' (Gambles: 1972.) A compact medium-jointed free-branching habit with well zoned, dark green leaves of medium size. The large flowerheads are held clear of the foliage on medium-length flower stems. Each bloom contains an abundance of bright crimson florets, and blooms can be produced at every leaf joint during the early season. Very free-flowering.

Perhaps not as good in the greenhouse as outdoors, where it is outstanding. Indoors it does tend to drop petals in hot conditions and like many single reds may scorch under glass when not properly shaded. Awarded a Silver Medal at the Vienna WIG 1974 exhibition.

5. 'Katrina' (Massheder: 1970.) A compact, short-jointed, medium-stemmed, free-branching variety that has average-sized, slightly zoned, mid-green, almost glossy leaves. Medium-length flower stems hold the large blooms clear of the foliage. The florets are a persian-rose colour with a small white eye, of good size and long pedicle; although there are not as many in each flowerhead as in some varieties, they seldom shatter. Floriferous.

Probably the first of his own seedlings that Guy Massheder introduced, it quickly achieved a regular position in the Top Ten. Another of those generous varieties that oblige with a flower at every node early in the season which, combined with its willingness to develop sideshoots and its reluctance to drop petals, makes it an excellent exhibition and garden variety. When grown specifically for a specimen cut bloom it can produce a very large flowerhead, but a bit of luck is needed to time it correctly.

6. 'Ashfield Serenade' (Keith Kidson: 1975.) A compact, dense, very short-jointed, self-branching habit with dark green, lightly zoned, soft and hairy leaves. A tetraploid. The short flower stems sometimes fail to clear the foliage during first flowering, so that the medium-size flowerheads are half hidden by leaves. The long-lasting florets are numerous, well formed on medium-length pedicles, pale lavender in colour.

It is difficult to imagine a basic zonal with a better growing habit, at least until it starts to flower. It is slow growing and unlikely to produce a large plant in its first year. It also tends to be a late flowerer and while not mean with flowers it is not over-generous. Once it has finished with those annoying first blooms hiding under leaves, it flowers and flowers without dropping, however, and without any need to stop or trim back the stems. It was the top single zonal in 1978 and 1979 so has given a lot of panellists a lot of pleasure.

Keith Kidson, incidentally, is an amateur grower living close to Ashfield Nurseries, and Guy Massheder apparently used to grow-on Keith's seedlings along with his own. They tell the story of the seedling that became 'Ashfield Serenade' developing rot close to the compost when very young. The rot was cut out and dusted but the plant looked very insecure so they bound the stem with Sellotape and forgot about it—it wasn't until after it had produced its first flower that they realised it was their 'stuck-up seedling'.

7. 'Dale Queen' (Roy & Joan Hinchcliffe: 1975.) A bushy, short-jointed, self-branching plant with dark green, zoned leaves of large size, soft and hairy. A tetraploid. The florets are of good size with long pedicles, a soft salmon-pink in colour. Very large flowerheads can be built up by the numerous pips and are supported by medium-to-long sturdy flower stems. Floriferous.

Yet another variety that had to achieve its initial success by enthusiasts passing on cuttings, before it was listed by Grey-bridge Geraniums. Roy and Joan Hinchcliffe are also from that Manchester area, which has produced almost as many amateur hybridists as it has varieties! A 'Regina' seedling, this variety has all the desirable characteristics of its illustrious parent but the individual floret perhaps lacks the perfection of form it might have had and it drops petals more readily than some varieties. However, although only one of many pink single-flowered 'Regina' seedlings, it has been the one to prevail and was the most popular in 1977 and second in 1978 and 1979, so that any minor criticism must be weighed against its overall excellence.

8. 'Highfield's Appleblossom' (Gambles: 1969.) Relatively slender-stemmed, short-jointed, branching habit with distinctive dark green, zoned leaves of medium size. Long flower stems just manage to hold the large flowerheads erect. Attractive florets of apple-blossom pink with an unusual salmon-pink eye, perfectly formed and long-lasting but not excessive in number. Floriferous.

Flowers early in the season, often from every node, and keeps flowering throughout the summer. Not a typical 'Gamble' zonal, it is quite distinctive, even when not in bloom. A beautiful and accommodating variety.

9. 'Christopher Ley' (Gambles: 1973.) A strong-growing, medium-to-long-jointed, sturdy-stemmed plant with mid-green, zoned leaves of above average size. The long, strong flower stems carry large blooms of large striking orange-red florets with darker veins on the upper petals. The florets also have a small white 'throat', are very flat and a perfect shape.

Not the easiest plant to grow to a good shape, but if well stopped it will accept training to a large bush, when the colour of the blooms provides a striking plant. Good for cut blooms, bedding and (given that little extra attention) exhibition purposes, especially when it produces flowers at every leaf joint as it often does early in its flowering season.

10. 'Highfield's Delight' (Gambles: 1969.) A compact, medium-jointed, branching variety with dark to mid-green, well zoned leaves. Medium-to-long flower stems hold the large flowerheads erect. The florets are well formed and a lovely shade of pale salmon. Very popular in the early 1970s it has not appeared in the Top Ten since 1976, although still favoured by several panellists.

11. 'Highfield's Perfecta' (Gambles: 1969.) A medium-jointed, branching variety with attractively zoned, mid-green leaves of average size. The medium-to-long flower stems hold good-sized blooms of large, well-formed florets in a charming coral-salmon colour.

A typical 'Gambles' single that was awarded a Bronze Medal at Vienna in 1974. It requires some stopping to encourage the denser, bushy habit for exhibition work. It has not appeared in the Top Ten since 1974 yet is still grown and shown by many exhibitors.

12. 'Pink Lady Harold' A strong, upright, long-jointed variety with large, zoned, mid-green leaves. The flush white florets with pink veins and centre are very large, of good shape and, with their long pedicle, build up into a large flowerhead on a long sturdy flower stem.

It has impressive flowers, but it requires a lot of attention if a good-shaped plant is to be obtained, as it appears to have a will of its own. Excellent for cut-bloom purposes, holding its petals well.

13. 'Highfield's Snowdrift' (Gambles: 1974.) A medium-jointed, strong-growing, sturdy-stemmed plant with medium-sized, light green leaves slightly zoned. The medium-to-long flower stems are (and have to be) strong to hold the large multi-pipped head. The large, well-formed florets are pure white.

We are told that a white zonal with a zone on the leaf will always display a touch of pink, yet this variety has shown little (if any) tendency to do so. It will often flower at every leaf joint when first blooming, but it tends to concentrate on flowers at the expense of foliage if attention is not paid to fertilizer. As in most white-flowered varieties the florets damp off when conditions are not right but it holds its petals well and warrants inclusion in any collection.

14. 'Highfield's Supreme' (Gambles: 1976.) A compact, medium-jointed, branching plant with mid-green, zoned leaves of good average size. The medium-length flower stems carry a well-formed flowerhead of many attractive, perfectly shaped, large florets in a cerise red with large white eye tending towards the upper two petals.

Although the overall bloom is not as large as in some varieties this can be more than made up for by the free-flowering habit; the 'Cyclops'-type floret must be one of the best produced in recent years. It will form a good bushy plant and is proving popular on the showbench.

15. 'Highfield's Choice' (Gambles: 1977.) A compact, bushy, short-jointed, self-branching plant with medium-sized, well-zoned, dark green leaves. A diploid. The short-to-medium flower stems hold the medium-sized, ball-shaped flowerheads easily and well clear of the foliage. The florets are of good size and shape in a pale lavender-pink. Very floriferous.

If there is another diploid, of this classification, with a growing habit even approaching the excellence of this variety it must be hiding somewhere. If 'Ashfield Serenade' has the near-perfect tetraploid habit, then 'Highfield's Choice' is its diploid counterpart among the basic zonals. One of the easiest plants to grow, it can produce flowers at every node during the first flush of flowers and continues to flower with minimum attention. It almost entered the Top Ten in its first full year and entered at number four in 1979.

Those then are the fifteen most popular varieties in this classification during the 1970s, but two of the 1979 Top Ten are not included, having been entered for the first time that year:
'Queen Ingrid' (Gambles: 1977.) A compact plant with short-to-medium joints and medium-thickness stem with medium, slightly zoned, mid-green leaves. Medium-length flower stems hold large flowerheads with large well-shaped florets of a true pink colour with a large white eye on the upper two petals. Floriferous.

The variety was named to honour a reputed geranium fan— Her Majesty Queen Ingrid of Denmark.
'May Rushbrook' (Gambles: 1975.) A compact, medium-jointed, branching variety having medium-sized leaves of mid-green colour only lightly zoned. The medium-to-large flowerheads top a medium-length flower stem with veined florets in a light, soft pink, and of good size and shape.

Named after the remarkable President of the Queensland Division of the Australian Geranium Society, who tirelessly chases after all things geranium on her visits to Britain and no doubt also when at home. This was always a potentially popular variety but took its time reaching the Top Ten.

In certain growing conditions most single-flowered zonals will drop petals, and this has only been mentioned if a variety is considered to depart from the norm. It is no coincidence that in 1979 three of the top four varieties in this classification were of excellent growing habit—this merely follows the regal and double-flowered zonal trend, and will be seen yet again when dwarf zonals are considered. There is no doubt that geraniums of naturally compact and bushy habit are easier to grow. They look better too. However, neither 'Ashfield Serenade' nor 'Highfield's Choice' have the most striking of flower colours, and almost certainly they will have been overtaken, probably by their own progeny of a similar habit but more positive colours, at the end of the 1980s. Hopefully, 'Highfield's Choice' is not a 'one-off fluke' and will pass on its best characteristics to its seedlings. We can already see the enthusiasts' natural preference for tetraploids, which will surely occupy at least half the Top Ten positions before long.

Also we shall be adjusting our thinking on what is 'short-jointed' for both single- and double-flowered zonals. In the mid-1960s, Irenes were described as short-jointed, but hardly anyone would call them so today. We may well be saying the same about 'Regina' and 'Dale Queen' as we enter the 1990s.

Without wishing to be repetitive, eleven out of the seventeen varieties described were raised at Gambles.

Single-flowered Zonals For Cut Bloom

As in the case of the double-flowered varieties, panellists are invited to select their favourites for cut-bloom purposes, under this classification, and the names of the top five are published each year. The combined results for the 1970s show the following seven as the most popular:

1. 'Kathleen Gamble'—see page 187.

2. 'Pride of the West' (Case: before 1910.) A strong-growing, long-jointed plant with medium-thickness stem and large mid-green leaves. The long flower stem holds a large flowerhead of large individual florets, rose-opal, flushed scarlet, with a white eye.

Almost certainly this reluctant-branching variety is grown solely for the size and beauty of the flower.

3. 'Pink Lady Harold'—see page 191.

4. 'Katrina'—see page 188.

5. 'Kingswood' (about 1910.) A strong-growing, long-jointed plant, medium-to-thick stemmed with large, mid-green, zoned leaves. Strong, long flower stems hold the large flowerheads very upright. The large individual florets have a large white eye strikingly displayed against a signal-red, the upper petals blending to fuchsia-purple.

Another plant grown principally for its flower, although it can be trained to a reasonable shape (particularly over two years). Also impressive as a bedder if occasionally stopped.

6. 'Dale Queen'—see page 189.

7. 'Staplegrove Fancy' (Case: about 1900.) An average-growing, medium-stemmed variety with medium-to-large, mid-green leaves. A long stem carries the large flowerhead, seldom overcrowded with pips, which are large of a white base colour and edged (usually blushed and dotted) with carmine-red, giving a picotee appearance.

A most unusual and attractive flower which, like the other two described in full in this section, has stood the test of time despite its difficult growing habits.

Pages 115–18 on growing cut blooms for exhibition dealt with the culture of plants for this section and further comment is unnecessary.

Green-leaved Zonal Geraniums For Bedding

Although this is not a formal classification for descriptive purposes, it is nevertheless important for practical purposes. The varieties selected by panellists as suitable for bedding are more easily considered together, rather than split into their individual specific classifications. There is no reason why dwarf or miniature varieties should not have been selected for this section by the panellists. The fact that none appears in the following list indicates that in fact insufficient panellists consider them ideal for bedding purposes.

The basic requirement of a good bedding zonal is that it should perform well over a long period in outdoor situations exposed to all of nature's elements. An additional implied requirement for those varieties described here is that they do all that in a British climate—an onerous requirement, and it is perhaps surprising we can find any to list! Indeed, this section can change noticeably from one year to the next, according to the amount of rain growers had to contend with each summer.

Both double- and single-flowered zonals for bedding are partially judged by how little they are damaged by wind and rain and how quickly they recover after any such damage. Frequently good bedding single-flowered varieties are (amusingly but probably correctly) described as 'self-cleansing' which, roughly translated, suggests they drop their petals readily—a characteristic considered to be detrimental in the past, and indeed it is—on *indoor* plants. This vice can, however, become a virtue in rainy conditions, though not in exposed windy situations. Semi-double varieties are lucky if they do not form a rather unsightly brown ball after heavy rain and it is best to remove the dead florets forming the ball as soon as possible to prevent following buds becoming affected by contact.

The results of the panellists' selections during the 1970s, when combined, indicate that the following seventeen have been the most consistently reliable. In view of the more noticeable change in choice in this section over ten years the position in the 1979 Top Ten is included where applicable.

1. 'Crampel's Master' (origination not known—but not recent). Strong-growing with upright sturdy *white* stems, long-jointed (particularly while flowering). Large, mid-green, zoned leaves with faint butterfly shading. The large flowerheads are held on long sturdy stems and are made up of a large number of *single* bright vermilion florets. (1979—3rd.)

An unusual and excellent bedding variety which unfortunately is downright frustrating under glass. The colour is identical to 'Paul Crampel', with that beautiful, almost fluorescent, appearance in the early evening. This variety is sometimes, somewhat optimistically, classified as an ornamental-leaved zonal (butterfly-leaved); it has attractive foliage certainly, but the markings are hardly distinct or consistent enough to justify anything other than the 'green-leaved' classification.

2. 'Treasure Chest'—see page 180 (1979—8th.)

3. 'Highfield's Pride'—see page 188 (1977-8-9—1st.)

4. 'King of Denmark' ('Beauté de Poitevine') (Bruant: 1877.) Average growing habit, thick-stemmed, medium-to-long-jointed with large mid-green, zoned leaves. The numerous flowerheads are supported by strong medium-to-long stems. The *semi-double* florets are a carmine-rose colour, the petals being variously marked with crimson veins.

This variety received an RHS Award of Merit in 1896 and has rightfully remained popular ever since.

5. 'Regina'—see page 176 (1979—5th.)

6. 'Red Glut' ('Dondo Red Glut'.) (Paul Schmid: early 1960s.)

A compact, short-jointed, medium-stemmed plant with medium-sized dark green leaves. The short-to-medium flower stems easily support the less than medium flowerheads which are produced in profusion. The *single* florets are an impressive deep red of medium size.

Apparently unlisted during the 1970s; in view of its popularity, it must have been passed from enthusiast to enthusiast. A pity, because this is a good low-growing variety that should be more readily available.

7. 'Highfield's Comet' (Gambles: 1969.) Average-growing, medium-stemmed, medium-jointed, branching habit. Medium-to-large leaves, mid-green in colour and zoned. The *single* florets are of average size and good shape forming a medium-sized flowerhead on a medium-to-long flower stem. The colour is a bright scarlet. (1979—9th.)

This variety was awarded a Bronze Medal at the Vienna WIG 1974 exhibition.

8. 'Zinc' (Neubonner Bros: 1922.) A compact, short-jointed, branching variety with dark green, zoned leaves of medium size. The *double* florets are bright scarlet and form a slightly less than medium flowerhead on medium-length stems. (1979—7th.)

Produces a continuous mass of bloom. Probably the most dwarf of the varieties in this section.

9. 'Zonnekind' (Mann, about 1960.) Average-growing, medium-stemmed, medium-jointed habit with mid-green, medium-sized leaves. The medium-sized flowerheads are made up of a good number of *single*, delicate pink florets held clear of the foliage on medium-length flower stems.

'Self-cleaning' outdoors, where it shrugs off the rain, but very much a 'dropper' in hot weather indoors. Not extensively listed.

10. 'Christopher Ley'—see page 190 (1979—6th.)

11. 'Decorator' ('Alphonse Ricard', 'President Baillet'.) (Bruant: 1894.) A strong-growing, long-jointed, thick-stemmed variety with large mid-green, zoned leaves. The *semi-double* (almost double) jasper-red florets, shaded vermilion, are numerous in each of the large flowerheads held on strong long stems.

A grand old variety that rewards the grower well, given a reasonably dry summer.

12. 'Maloja' (Hartmann: c1960.) A compact, bushy, medium-jointed, average-stemmed plant with medium-sized, mid-green leaves. The large flowerheads of *single* orange-red florets are well supported on medium-length flower stems. Free-flowering.

One of the most reliable of bedding geraniums in any summer, wet or dry.

13. 'Ashfield Monarch'—see page 179 (1979—2nd.)

14. 'Springtime'—see page 180 (1979—10th.)

15. 'Paul Crampel' (Lemoine: 1892.) A long-jointed (by today's standards), medium-stemmed variety with well zoned, dark-to-mid-green leaves of good size. The large flowerheads are held on long strong (enough) stems and are made up of a mass of *single* florets, a bright vermilion in colour with darker veins. Free-flowering.

Whether the original 'Paul Crampel' is still available is uncertain, as never was a name so plagiarized—everyone who grew a red seedling for sale called it by this name which guaranteed its commercial success. Perhaps the most popular geranium of the century and the bedrock of most park and formal garden displays before and after World War I. Perhaps even more than 'Crampel's Master' it has a fluorescent appearance in early evening light, and in a massed display must be difficult to better.

16. 'Henry Weller' (Gambles: 1970.) Compact, medium-jointed, medium-stemmed plant with medium-to-large, mid-green, well zoned leaves. The medium-to-large flowerheads are held on a strong, medium-length stems, with the *single* well-shaped, coral-salmon florets resisting dropping more than most.

Named after perhaps the most knowledgeable and enthusiastic amateur geranium fanatic the author has been privileged to meet—with a record on the showbench that proves he can grow them as well as he knows them. Originally included in Gamble's display at Chelsea in 1969.

17. 'Ashfield Blaze' (Kidson: 1977.) A compact, bushy, short-jointed, thick-stemmed plant with dark green, zoned leaves of medium-to-large size. A tetraploid. The flowerheads are medium-to-large in size on a sturdy medium-length stem. The *semi-double* florets are numerous with good-length pedicles and have an unusual scarlet colour suggesting orange overtones with paler reverse. Free-flowering. (1979—4th.)

Actually introduced at Southport Show on a BEGS display two years after Ashfield Nursery had ceased trading—may sadly prove to be the last 'Ashfield' variety. Should be a good pot plant but not quite as outstanding as when planted in the open.

That completes the list of popular bedding zonals, which does not include a single F1 hybrid. With the remarkable proliferation of available F1 varieties in the late 1970s, it is unlikely that at least a couple will not establish themselves as popular bedding varieties during the 1980s. They are already commercially popular but whether this is because the public is demanding them or because the vast majority of bedding varieties offered for sale to the general public (as opposed to specialist growers) are F1 hybrids—we shall have to wait to find out.

Dwarf Zonals

This group of zonals is classified by the size of the plants. Being the group between basic and miniature there are obviously likely to be differences of opinion among growers about varieties at both ends of the imposed specifications.

A dwarf zonal is generally accepted as such if its foliage exceeds 5 in but is not over 8 inches in height on a fully grown plant. In practice any variety that is happy (it will be obvious if it isn't) growing in a $4\frac{1}{2}$ in pot and remains within that height limitation can be regarded as a dwarf. There are other limitations requiring the leaves, flowerheads and florets to be proportionate to the size of the plant, and in their own way these requirements can be as important in classifying the habit as the height itself.

The plant in bloom must look right, and this is the real criterion for deciding whether you should grow it as a dwarf or as a basic or miniature. Experiment if you are in doubt by growing two similar plants, one as a dwarf and the other as a basic or a miniature, whichever is the more suitable. Once both plants are in bloom it is usually clear whether they are dwarf by nature or better as the selected alternative. Not even natural dwarf varieties are necessarily entirely proportionate, as they may have one or more feature(s) that do not truly conform. Although there was an occasional 'one-off' dwarf before 1950, that particular year appears to have been the starting point for modern-style dwarf zonals. Four prominent hybridists all introduced dwarf varieties around that time—three Americans, Milton Arndt ('Epsilon'), Ernest Rober ('Rober's Lavender') and Holmes Miller ('Imp'); and Frank G. Read of Norfolk, England ('Dwarf Miriam Basey'). It would, however, be wrong to overlook two varieties that appeared in Holland some five years previously, 'Emma Hossler' and 'Mr Everatts', which are as proportionately correct as dwarf varieties are expected to be some 35 years afterwards. The breeding of dwarf varieties has continued at breakneck speed in both the USA and Europe. Mr Miller and Mr Read were subsequently joined by Messrs G. T. Hill, H. F. Parrett, S. Peat, T. Portas and R. C. Bidwell in Britain, while in the USA E. H. Eisley, Wilson Bros and Mrs Bruce Crane all kept the momentum going. The Rev Stanley Stringer may have topped them all with many of his 'Deacon' varieties, five of which feature in the combined Top Ten of the 1970s. As previously suggested these varieties may prove of more lasting influence than the breathtaking 'Regina'. The 'Deacons', or at least the best of them—for they are not all possessed of the almost ideal habit of 'Deacon Lilac Mist'—do seem to meet the demands of our times, certainly in the UK. They are suitable for smaller gardens, ornamental patio tubs, window boxes, 8 ft by 6 ft greenhouses and, probably most importantly, those ridiculous narrow windowsills we now have to tolerate.

Almost all the dwarf single-flowered varieties and many of the double-flowered are excellent outdoor plants, while conversely all the double-flowered and many of the single-flowered varieties are excellent indoors, either in greenhouse or home, given good light.

There are currently at least ten distinct classifications for dwarf zonals, green, gold, bicolour and tricolour foliages all being represented; and each of these four has both single-flowered and double/semi-double alternatives. The remaining two classifications are cactus-flowered varieties in green-leaf and bicolour-leaf types. Panellists are not asked to differentiate between suitable greenhouse and bedding varieties when selecting their favourites but they have probably tended to select with greenhouse cultivation in mind. Their combined 1970s selections resulted in the following varieties proving the most popular. Note that the terms medium, large, small, short and the like should all be regarded as describing dwarf plants, thus medium (dwarf) leaf, large (dwarf) floret.

1. 'Deacon Lilac Mist' (Rev S. Stringer: 1970.) A compact, dense, short-jointed, self-branching, thin-to-medium-stemmed plant with dark green, zoned leaves of medium-to-large size.

The medium flower heads are held erect on sturdy medium-length stems and are made up of a not excessive number of large double florets of pale lilac colour with a paler reverse to the petals.

'Deacons' have been described as 'floribunda geraniums' and that is a good description, as once they begin to flower there are usually two blooms to each stem at any one time—one coming and one going. This particular variety has probably the best habit of the first twelve released (we have hardly had an opportunity to assess the last dozen) and was one of the original six exhibited initially at Chelsea Flower Show in 1970 by Wyck Hill Geraniums. If this variety (and the other 'Deacons') has a fault it is that the individual florets are a little large for a dwarf, but this is counteracted as they do not form a very large head. The first dwarf choice of panellists each year from 1973.

2. 'Emma Hossler' (May have been raised by Anders—it was certainly in Holland c1945.) A medium-jointed, branching, thin-stemmed variety with medium-sized, pale-to-mid-green leaves. Medium-length flower stems hold medium-sized flowerheads of average-sized double florets, of pale rose-pink with a small white throat.

A true dwarf that you will have little difficulty keeping in shape and proportionate, with minimal stopping.

3. 'Deacon Minuet' (Stringer: 1973.) A dense, medium-to-long-jointed, medium-stemmed, branching variety with large, dark green leaves with deep, broad zone. The medium-to-long flower stems support average-sized flowerheads of medium-to-large double florets in an attractive two-tone pale pink.

This variety will require stopping to keep below 8 in but is well worth the effort, having the best foliage of the first dozen 'Deacons'. It is the only variety to reach the Top Ten from the second six released in 1973, although the white-flowered 'Deacon Arlon', released at the same time, has been close on more than one occasion.

4. 'Deacon Romance' (Stringer: 1970.) Bushy, medium-jointed, branching, medium-stemmed habit with medium-to-large dark green leaves. The well-shaped medium-sized flowerheads are held erect on medium-length flower stems. Medium-to-large fully double florets, a deep neon-pink in colour.

An excellent pot variety but perhaps a little too double to give of its best outdoors.

5. 'Deacon Bonanza' (Stringer: 1970.) A bushy, medium-jointed, branching, medium-stemmed, spreading habit with large, dark green leaves. The medium flower stems hold the largish flowerheads erect. The large 'neyron-rose' (pale magenta-pink) with paler reverse double florets are not too numerous in each bloom.

Floriferous, growing well in almost any situation.

6. 'Deacon Fireball' (Stringer: 1970.) A low-growing, spreading, medium-jointed, medium-stemmed habit with medium-to-large, well-zoned dark green leaves. The rather outward-growing large flowerheads are held on longish flower stems. The double florets are large and an excellent scarlet colour.

It did not achieve Top Ten status until 1975, perhaps because of its tendency to throw its blooms sideways like spokes from the hub of a wheel. This can be corrected by stopping and tying before (and even during) flowering. A better bedder than you might expect.

7. 'Pink Champagne' ('Walter Dietzman') (Walter Dietzman: a 1947 sport from 'Radio'.) This variety is identical to its forebear (see 8 below) apart from the beautiful silvery-pink flower colouring.

These two varieties were very popular in the late 1960s and early 1970s, and justifiably so. They are amazingly floriferous, covering themselves in bloom for long periods, but they do tend to forget they have leaves to support as well, and high nitrogen feeding is recommended. The flowerheads also have a mutated crown in many cases—the florets seem to grow away from two or more centres. The overall effect is not spoiled by this but they would never make an exhibition cut bloom. The self-branching characteristic also gives the frequent impression of a mutation, as the stem divides rather than forming sideshoots.

8. 'Salmon Supreme' ('Radio') (Anders: 1935.) Strong-growing, medium-jointed, medium-stemmed, self-branching plants with medium to large mid-green leaves. Rather untidy medium-to-large flowerheads are held on medium-length flower stems. The semi-double florets are a deep (almost red) salmon of medium size. Very floriferous.

This variety has undoubtedly been used in breeding programmes throughout Europe and the USA particularly during the 1940s and 1950s and may have played a part in many of the popular varieties we grow today.

9. 'Fantasie' ('Fantasia') (origination not known.) A bushy, dense, medium-jointed, thin-stemmed, branching habit with medium-sized pale to mid-green leaves. The short-to-medium-length flower stems hold the average-sized blooms sufficiently clear of the foliage to produce a good overall effect yet still allow the almost-double pure white medium-to-large florets to contrast against the leaves. Free-flowering.

The origins of this plant are doubtful, although it was certainly available in the late 1960s and may even be an improved stock of 'Dick's White'. The white florets have that green tint that always seems to signify the flower won't 'pink'. It will repay tenfold the time spent stopping and training and should be included in every dwarf zonal collection.

10. 'Morval' (Portas: 1976.) A compact, dense, self-branching, thin- to-medium-stemmed, short-jointed habit with medium-to-large, golden chestnut zoned leaves. The medium-length flower stems hold the average-sized flowerheads perfectly erect above the foliage. The large double blush-pink florets are sufficient in number to provide long-lasting blooms but not too many to create too large a flowerhead. Free-flowering.

Named after the Cornish village, visited by Arthur (and Jane) Biggin, BEGS's long-serving secretary. It just missed Top Ten status in its first full year and has been second to 'Deacon Lilac Mist' in 1978 and 1979. A real all-purpose geranium; its attractive golden foliage earns it the distinction of being the only variety to be in two Top Ten lists, for different classifications during the 1970s.

11. 'Wendy Read' (Frank G. Read: 1974.) Compact, dense, short-jointed, branching, thin-to-medium-stemmed habit with medium-sized dark green leaves. The medium-sized flowerheads on short-to-medium stems are held erect. The double deep rose-pink, shading to blush-white, florets are of medium-to-large size. Free-flowering.

This is an excellent variety, although anyone familiar with Mr Read's 'Norfolk strain' would not recognize this, nor the following variety, as a 'Read' plant. They display the characteristics of the best 'Deacons' rather than the stronger, more erect, darker leaf habit of the earlier varieties released by Mr Read, most of which require effort to keep down to 8 in and achieve a real breadth to the plant, although their other charms compensate.

12. 'Emma Jane Read' (Read: 1975.) Another compact, bushy, short-jointed, branching, thin- to-medium-stemmed plant with medium-sized dark green leaves. Medium-sized flowerheads top an average-length stem and the double, medium-sized florets of a deep mauve-pink form a well-shaped and attractive bloom.

Another grand variety, perhaps a little more fickle and temperamental than her sister (above) but not difficult.

13. 'Dwarf Miriam Basey' (Read: 1950.) Compact, short-jointed, branching, medium-stemmed habit tending to grow rather erect, with very dark green, medium-sized leaves. The erect, medium-to-long flower stems support largish flowerheads of *single*, large-sized florets of good shape. The colour is either white, edged/flushed cherry-red or an inconsistent cherry-red with an irregular white central eye (take your pick).

One of Mr Read's original releases, and popularly held to be the first British dwarf. It is the only single-flowered variety to merit inclusion here and, being an old and cherished friend, can be recommended for inclusion in any geranium collection—a beautiful sight in full flower and it will perform well anywhere if well fed.

14. 'Tammy' (May: 1965.) A tall-growing, medium- to-long-jointed, thin-stemmed variety with pale green, lightly zoned, medium-sized leaves. Longish flower stems hold medium to large flowerheads with a good number of large double florets in a bright scarlet.

This one will remain popular until the hybridists manage to reproduce the excellent flower colour on a more compact plant.

Once again, varieties with a better growing habit have emerged strongly. Indeed, if reluctant criticism were to be levelled at many of the grossly underpraised (probably underpaid) specialist geranium nurseries it would be that they tend to regard 'dwarf' as a sufficient catalogue description of a plant's habit. There are of course good, average and indifferent dwarf (and miniature) growing habits, just as there are for basic zonal varieties. After the great progress made in the thirty years from 1950, future development may well concentrate on improving the existing selection rather than bring remarkable breakthroughs, although the innovations produced by hybridists remain a continual source of amazement.

Miniature Zonals

Miniature zonal geraniums have long been accepted, in Britain at least, as varieties which do not exceed 5 inches in height of foliage when fully grown. To this should be added the provision that the leaves, flowerheads and florets should be proportionate to a plant of that size. As with dwarf zonals, perfection has proved difficult to achieve, particularly in keeping down the size of florets, and consequently flowerheads, to a proportionate size; but great progress has been made by a handful of hybridists. Almost all the breeders of dwarf varieties, mentioned in the last section, have contributed to the miniature section, but particularly the Rev S. Stringer and Messrs Miller, Parrett and Bidwell. The last-mentioned has also specialised commercially in all types of dwarf and miniature geraniums and produces an extensive catalogue, as 'East Anglian Specialist', offering over 300 varieties of such plants.

The uses of miniature zonals are limited by their size, although the right varieties in the right situations will perform as well as any of their larger relations, either in the open ground or in pots and other containers. They are principally novelty plants of immense charm and interest, obviously useful in particular situations demanding small plants, as well as being ideally suited to geranium enthusiasts with limited space. Eight or nine of these miniatures can be grown on the bench space required by a single plant of 'Regina'.

The culture of these varieties is identical to that of full-sized plants, although obviously greater care has to be taken when handling the miniatures, and propagating, stopping, tying, removing dying or dead leaves and stipules, and even straightforward watering and feeding are more fiddling (and important). All these plants should be capable of performing well in $3\frac{1}{2}$ in pots but that means very little compost, so that watering, feeding and general attention are inevitably required more frequently.

Nature itself, with the help of an attentive plantsman, probably produced the breakthrough(s) that led to the extensive range of miniatures now available. The modern miniature zonal can probably be traced back to 'Red Black Vesuvius' in 1889, which the author has been brought up to believe arose from a sport of 'Vesuvius', a basic bedding variety of the period. Very shortly afterwards Lemoine, in France, introduced 'Mme Fournier', but whether this was entirely independent or related to 'Red Black Vesuvius' we do not know. Their distinctive, almost black, leaves can still be recognized today in most popular miniature zonals, and in the absence of more definitive detective work this suggested origin is probably as reliable as any other you have been given in this book!

Currently there are five distinct classifications available in miniature zonals. Green, gold, bicolour and tricolour foliage are all available with single flowers, but only the green-leaved types have double flowers (at present). Some people may suggest that some of the double flowers are really rosebud and they will find no disagreement here, although others who think this is only because the smaller, more compact, florets merely look as if they have a greater number of petals are equally entitled to that opinion. As with the dwarf zonals, the panellists are asked for their selections on a general basis, no distinction being made between greenhouse and bedding varieties, although the predominance of double-flowered varieties probably indicates the preference for growing these plants in pots. Here are the overall results from the 1970 lists. As for dwarf varieties, descriptive terms for sizes refer to what is expected for miniatures: thus medium (miniature) leaf; large (miniature) floret.

1. 'Jane Eyre' (Stringer: 1970.) A compact, dense, medium-jointed, self-branching, medium-stemmed habit with medium-to-large, glossy, dark green, zoned leaves. Medium-to-large flowerheads are held on short stems. The medium-to-large double florets are a deep lavender colour.

It reached the number one position in the second year the lists were published, and has consistently held that position since. An excellent variety, easy to grow (for a miniature) and beautiful in flower, although not the most prolific bloomer and takes longer than most to flower after its final stop.

2. 'Keepsake' (Miller: 1962.) Bushy, tending to be erect, medium-to-long-jointed, branching, medium-to-thick-stemmed plant with medium-to-dark green, slightly zoned leaves of average size. The longish flower stems support large flowerheads made up of large double florets in an attractive rosy-purple colour with an irregular white centre.

Requires stopping to create a bushy effect and is a borderline miniature/dwarf, but flowers well.

3. 'Orion' (Stringer: 1965.) Compact, small-to-medium-jointed, thin-to-medium-stemmed, self-branching habit with medium-sized, dark green lightly zoned leaves. The medium-length flower stems hold the average-sized flowerheads erect above the foliage. The medium-sized fully double florets are a lovely orange-red colour.

A natural and genuine miniature that is easier to grow and propagate than most. An early-season bloomer, although petals tend to drop in hot weather.

4. 'Grace Wells' (W. Wells: 1963.) Compact, dense, medium-stemmed, medium-jointed, branching habit with medium-to-large, dark green, faintly zoned leaves. Medium flower stems with large flowerheads held erect. The large single florets are of good shape in a veined pale mauve colour with a small white eye on the two upper petals.

Another natural miniature and certainly the best of the single-flowered varieties.

5. 'Margery Stimpson' (H. F. Parrett: 1968.) Strong, erect, thick-stemmed, long-jointed habit with large, dark green leaves. The medium-to-long flower stems hold the largish flowerheads erect. The large double florets of shaded amaranth-rose are truly beautiful in their own right.

This variety requires a lot of attention to keep it below 5 in and to encourage it to bush out, but if you can spare the time it will result in one of the most beautiful miniature plants.

6. 'Francis Parrett' (Parrett: 1968.) Sturdy, medium-to-long-jointed, rather erect medium-to-thick stems with medium-sized, mid-green leaves. The sturdy medium-length flower stem holds the medium-sized flowerheads erect and well clear of the foliage. Medium-sized fully double florets of bright lavender colour form a dense ball-like head.

Another variety that will repay regular stopping in the early months to encourage branching.

7. 'Cheiko' (Parrett: 1968.) A dense, compact plant, medium-jointed, medium-to-thick-stemmed, self-branching with medium-to-large, mid-green leaves. Medium-to-long, sturdy flower stems hold the largish flowerheads erect. The double florets are large in an unusual and attractive colour combination of crimson and purple (plum-red effect).

An excellent variety that flowers a little later than many others but a real eyecatcher when in flower. Easy to grow.

8. 'Rosita' (May: 1965.) A compact, medium-jointed, branching, medium-to-thin-stemmed habit with average-sized mid-to-dark green, zoned leaves. Medium-length flower stems support the largish ball-shaped blooms directly above the foliage. The very tight double florets are not too large and the bright crimson colour would be welcome on any size plant.

A 'rosebud' description for this variety would be unlikely to infringe the Trades Descriptions Act. Remarkably easy to grow if not always to propagate.

9. 'Royal Norfolk' (Stringer: 1976.) Sturdy, dense, branching from medium-thick stems of medium joints with average to large, dark green leaves. The short sturdy flower stems hold the large blooms clear of the foliage. The large, intense rose-purple florets are double.

A relative newcomer to the Top Ten lists that has already been as high as second place. It requires taming if it is not to exceed 5 in but is impressive when in bloom.

10. 'Martin Parrett' (Parrett: 1970.) Virtually identical in habit to 'Francis Parrett' (above), only the distinct rose-pink colour of the florets being different.

11. 'Timothy Clifford' (Burrows: 1955.) A compact, bushy, short-jointed, medium-stemmed variety with small- to medium-sized, dark green, well zoned leaves. The medium-length flower stems hold the blooms erect. The double slightly furled petals are a delightful salmon-pink with subtle tones, not too large and forming a ball-like flowerhead. Free-flowering.

One of the author's very first varieties and certainly his first miniature—so beware sentimental bias. A true miniature, easy to grow and propagate with a most attractive flower that stands out in any company, despite its size.

12. 'Miss Wackles' (Stringer: 1970.) A sturdy, erect, medium- to long-jointed, thickish-stemmed variety with large, dark green leaves. The medium-length flower stem gives good support to large flowerheads. The double florets, almost too large, have a deep red colour.

A most impressive colour, but the plant requires attention to achieve a good shape and to prevent it growing too tall.

13. 'Claydon' (R. C. Bidwell: 1970.) A compact, bushy, self-branching, short-jointed, thin-to-medium-stemmed habit with medium-sized, dark green, well zoned leaves. The short-to-medium-length flower stems hold the average-sized flowerheads erect above the foliage. The medium-sized, rather untidy, semi-double florets are an attractive lavender-pink in colour. Very prolific.

It entered the lists for the first time in 1979—at number two. Very appealing in both foliage and flower, this will almost certainly prove a good exhibition variety.

14. 'Fleurette' (Case: 1955.) A sturdy, erect, long-jointed, thick-stemmed variety with medium-to-large dark green leaves. Medium-length sturdy, flower stems topped by medium-to-large flowerheads. The large double florets are a good deep pink.

A 'big' miniature that requires plenty of stops to obtain an exhibition shape and keep within the acceptable height.

15. 'Sunstar' (Stringer: 1967.) Short, dense, medium-jointed, branching, medium-stemmed habit with unusually heavily lobed, medium-sized, mid-green leaves. The medium-to-large flowerhead of large, double bright-orange florets is held on a longish flower stem.

A remarkably true miniature version of the basic zonal variety 'Orangesonne'.

Those fifteen varieties offer a wide selection but are rather heavily weighted towards the lavender/mauve/purple flower colours, perhaps because these colours do tend to go with good growing habits. There is no white in the top fifteen, and although having a pink effect 'Belinda Adams' might remedy that omission.

Yet again many varieties with beautiful flowers appear to have been relegated by panellists in favour of those with good but less spectacular flowers but superior plant habit. Despite this, many catalogues—with a couple of notable exceptions—give no information about a variety's growing habit, merely classifying the floret as single or double and describing the colour. This is done not just with miniature zonals but with most types of geranium, and despite the obvious extra printing costs it would surely be worth giving growers even a mere two or three words on plant habit.

There has been a tendency for larger blooms on miniatures in recent years, with a corresponding tendency by exhibition judges not to penalize this fault in proportion. These tendencies are unfortunate, as the true beauty of dwarf and miniature varieties surely lies in all the characteristics of the plants being uniformly reduced. No ornamental-leaved varieties appear among the panellists' selections, but it would be surprising if gold-leaved varieties, at least, do not invade this list during the next five years.

Having now covered the three principal habit classifications for zonal geraniums we will conclude the lists with three sections on these 'ornamental-leaved' types which are distinctive enough in their own right to transcend the 'habit' classifications.

Gold-leaved Zonals

This type of zonal geranium is classified by the colour of its foliage. It includes all those varieties with leaves that range from pale yellow, with or without a zone, to dark golden or near-green and those with leaves with a very broad prominent zone giving the 'bronzed' effect.

As already mentioned, gold-leaved types appear under all three plant-habit classifications, in two instances with both single and double or semi-double flowers. There are currently five classifications available with gold leaves: basic gold-leaved single-flowered, basic gold-leaved double (semi-double) flowered, dwarf gold-leaved single-flowered, dwarf gold-leaved double (semi-double) flowered and miniature gold-leaved single-flowered. It can surely not be long before Mr Bidwell produces the golden-leaved double-flowered miniature to complete the set! It goes without saying that all the above are zonal types.

Gold-leaved plants developed almost by accident with the occasional new variety appearing from time to time, until Sam Peat of Bristol and Tom Portas of Leicester began deliberately to explore the possibilities of this section. Great strides were made in the 1970s, particularly with the double/semi-double varieties, as the listed varieties will show. The previous loose and totally inadequate inclusion of this classification among 'ornamental-leaved varieties' became ludicrous, as the new varieties not only demanded their own classification but began to swamp the bicolours and tricolours by weight of number.

Gold-leaved varieties include many that are suitable for bedding purposes and many that are best grown under cover, with the occasional all-rounders that seem to perform well in any situation. Wherever they are grown they provide an ideal contrast with green-leaved neighbours. Most, but as usual not all, such varieties have a tendency to be slow-growing, almost dwarf, in habit which is an admirable characteristic and makes many of the varieties suitable for growing in a light position in the home, where their lovely foliage will brighten any room, whether the plant is in or out of flower.

Panellists are asked to select gold-leaved varieties separately for greenhouse and for bedding purposes and the top five of each section are published annually. The following varieties are those that have been most successful in their respective sections during the 1970s.

GREENHOUSE VARIETIES

1. 'Jubilee' (c1890.) Strong growing, medium-jointed, medium-stemmed habit with medium-to-large leaves only slightly golden but with a most prominent broad bronze zone. The small-to-medium flowerheads are held clear of the foliage on medium-length flower stems. The small single florets are a pale salmon colour.

Perhaps the best example of the 'bronze-leaved' type, having a most striking leaf which certainly accounts for its number one position in this section; the flowers are insignificant by comparison. Almost certainly introduced to coincide with one of Queen Victoria's Jubilees—it would be appropriate if it were the Golden Jubilee.

2. 'Richard Key' (Sam Peat: 1970.) Compact, short-jointed, spreading, branching habit with medium-sized leaves of a yellow-gold colour lightly zoned. The small-to-medium flowerheads are easily held erect above the foliage by short stems. Double florets in a pale mauve colour give an unusual and pleasing effect against the foliage. Free-flowering.

Named after the son of the proprietors of Greybridge Geraniums (who have introduced almost all of Sam Peat's seedlings). A very easy variety to grow well. In addition to producing new varieties, Sam Peat has been involved in setting up a flourishing geranium society based around Bristol.

3. 'Boudoir' (Peat: 1973.) A bushy, short-jointed, branching plant with medium-sized, light gold leaves with an irregular zone. The short flower stems hold the small-to-medium flowerheads clear of the foliage. The florets are double, of a lavender-pink colour, but relatively few appear in each flowerhead.

Another easy-to-grow variety (once rooted) that requires minimal stopping. It has performed well in outdoor tubs.

4. 'Ursula Key' (Peat: 1968.) A compact, short-jointed, low-growing branching variety with medium-sized, gold leaves that have a distinct chestnut zone. The short flower stems hold small-to-medium flowerheads of double coral-salmon florets. Free-flowering. Named after Richard's sister.

5. 'Jane Biggin' (Portas: 1976.) A low-growing, short-jointed habit with dense, medium-sized, bright yellow-gold leaves with distinct light broad zone. The short-to-medium flower stems support small-to-medium flowerheads with a good number of double florets in a delightful strawberry-pink. Free-flowering.

Named after the long-suffering wife of Arthur Biggin, under whose secretaryship (and Dennis Fielding's chairmanship) the British & European Geranium Society has grown to a 2,000 membership in ten years. This variety is so compact and dense, invariably carrying two blooms on each stem at the same time, that it appears to have more branches than are actually there. Consequently a bit mean in providing cuttings.

6. 'Morval'—see page 202.

BEDDING VARIETIES

1. 'Mrs Quilter' (Laing: 1880.) A compact, naturally well-shaped, short-jointed, thin-stemmed habit with small-to-medium-sized, gold-green leaves and broad deep chestnut zone. The medium-length flower stems carry small-to-medium flowerheads of small, single florets of porcelain-rose.

This variety has also appeared in the top five greenhouse varieties and makes one of the tidiest, shapeliest plants available. Unfortunately the almost insignificant flowers restrict its show-bench appearances, though it has surprised a few flashier varieties on occasions.

2. 'Marechal MacMahon' (Cannell: 1872.) Another compact, short-jointed, thin stemmed variety with small-to-medium leaves having a very uniform, broad, almost mahogany zone on a pod-green base. The flower stems are of medium length carrying a small-to-medium-size flowerhead of small single vermilion florets.

Awarded an RHS First Class Certificate in 1872. Named after the President of the Third Republic of France. Very similar to 'Mrs Quilter' but slightly more open and with a superior zoning.

3. 'Jubilee'—see page 210.

4. 'Patsy Q' (Portas: 1975.) A bushy, medium-jointed, medium-stemmed habit with medium-sized, gold leaves and good purple-chestnut zone. Medium-to-long flower stems carry good-sized flowerheads of largish single salmon-pink florets.

Also an excellent pot plant (1979–5th). Will produce a large specimen plant with reasonable attention and like 'Susie Q' (No 7), should remain popular for many years to come.

5. 'Copper Flair' (Harold Bagust: 1966.) A compact, medium-jointed medium-stemmed habit with medium-to-large, pale green leaves which display a uniform, broad deep-copper zone. The medium-length flower stems carry quite large, well-shaped blooms of many single salmon-peach florets.

Mr Bagust was the proprietor of Wyck Hill Geraniums and this is a reputed cross between 'Prince Regent' and 'Jubilee'. A very attractive bedding variety.

6. 'Golden Crest' (Harrison: 1960.) A bushy, medium-jointed, medium-stemmed branching variety with medium-sized, crinkled, golden (tending to green) leaves. The medium-length flower stems carry average-sized flowerheads of single salmon flowers.

7. 'Susie Q' (Portas: 1976.) A compact, short-to-medium-jointed, medium-stemmed, branching variety with medium-size gold leaves and light bronze zone. Medium-length flower stems with medium-to-large flowerheads of soft pink, well-formed single florets.

Perhaps a slightly better habit than 'Patsy Q' (above) and even better as an exhibition variety when grown in a pot in the greenhouse (1979—4th).

The rapid improvement in this classification may sadly not continue following Tom Portas's death in 1980. Many of his later varieties, however, are just becoming known in the 1980s and some of these may displace a few of the previous favourites described in this chapter. Almost certainly we shall see the miniature golden-leaved zonal range extended, with improved single-flowered varieties as well as the awaited double-flowered breakthrough.

Bicolour Zonals

The true origins of bicolour (and tricolour) varieties are not known and probably arose from more than one quirk of nature. Developments from the mid-nineteenth century are clearer, thanks to Peter Grieve's *A History of Ornamental Foliaged Pelargoniums with Practical Hints for Their Production, Propagation and Cultivation*, the second edition of which has recently been republished by the British Pelargonium and Geranium Society, thanks to a legacy from Miss Mary Campbell. From around 1850 the popularity and breeding of ornamental-leaved zonal geraniums apparently knew no bounds and many more varieties were available at that time than there are today. It is impossible to identify some of the older varieties that still exist, but we can happily enough accept the names currently available, even if they may not all have stayed with the same variety throughout the last hundred years.

The bicolour zonal sub-classification is used under basic, dwarf and miniature classifications and within the first two sections has both single- and double-flowered forms, but only single-flowered miniatures. There is also at least one cactus-flowered bicolour variety (see page 220). The cultivation is no different from that of green-leaved varieties but, almost without exception, bicolour and tricolour varieties are more erect and slower-growing and, therefore, need more stopping and training over a longer period to achieve specimen-plant status. Second-year plants at about 15 to 18 months are usually ideal.

Panellists are asked to select bicolour zonals on a greenhouse-only basis and bicolours and tricolours together on a bedding basis. The following varieties are the most popular bicolour selections from both lists during the 1970s.

GREENHOUSE VARIETIES

1. 'Frank Headley' (Frank Headley: c1957.) A dwarf, compact, thin-stemmed medium-jointed variety, with small-to-medium silver/white-edged leaves occasionally faintly zoned. The long flower stems hold the sparse, open flowerheads erect and well above the foliage. The single, primitive florets are a pleasant dawn-pink. One of the most prolific-flowering varieties.

A truly 'all-purpose' geranium, a must for every collection. It may not have achieved Overall Top Ten status until it had come of age in 1978, but it fully deserves that exalted position. Although naturally a dwarf with reasonable but not excessive stopping, it can be grown on for three or four years with trimming (rather than cutting-back) to form a large specimen plant

213

topped by a mass of flowerheads fighting for space. Perhaps it drops petals a little too readily but there are so many of them it hardly matters. This one will even perform well in mid-winter, if grown specifically for that purpose, and makes a lovely centre-piece for the Christmas dinner table. If it isn't obvious already, *we* like this one!

2. 'Freak of Nature' (Gray: 1880.) A slow-growing basic type, compact, rather erect, medium-jointed and stemmed habit with medium-to-large-sized ivory leaves having bright green wavy-ruffled edges. The average-length white flower stems (leaf and main stems are white too) hold the medium-sized flowerheads erect. The single vermilion florets are well shaped (for an ornamental-leaved variety) and combine to form a very acceptable bloom.

This variety was well named by Mr Gray, and should be welcomed by ordinary geranium growers and religious fanatics alike, as those clever geneticists will shamefacedly inform us that such a leaf colouring is impossible! In fairness it must be added that no one has yet repeated Mr Gray's achievement in reversing the normal green/white colourings. Please don't assume this variety is merely a novelty, however, as although the flowers are not prolific they present a delightful contrast to the leaves and a well-trained plant is a joy to behold.

3. 'Mont Blanc' (Cannell: 1900.) Another slow-growing basic type, compact, erect, medium-to-short-jointed, medium-to-thin-stemmed variety with small-to-medium-sized bright mid-green, silver white-edged leaves. The average-length flower stems easily support the small but full flowerheads above the foliage. The small, single, well-shaped florets are a dull but pure white colour.

Rediscovered among Don Stilwell's collection of geraniums while he was still a top amateur exhibitor (ie, pre-Woodbridge Nursery, who, along with Greybridge Geraniums, have recently listed this variety). The origins may be unknown but to have achieved Top Five status while still unlisted speaks for its striking appearance.

4. 'Rene Roue' (Don Storey: 1973.) A basic, compact, erect, medium-jointed, medium-stemmed plant, with medium-sized green-edged white leaves. The short-to-medium flower stems are topped by well-shaped, medium-sized flowerheads. The average-sized single florets are a bright red in colour.

Apparently not currently listed but an excellent variety for all that. Slow-growing and requires training, but it will produce an excellent plant if well looked after.

5. 'Mrs (J. C.) Mappin' (Townsend: 1880.) A basic type, erect but bushy, medium-jointed and stemmed variety with small-to-medium, silvery-grey-green/pale yellow-white-edged leaves. The medium-length flower stems support medium-sized, infrequent but well-shaped flowerheads. The medium-sized single florets are a very pale pink-lavender (almost white) veined colour with darker (almost vermilion) centre.

A very acceptable variety, easily grown and propagated, but a little short on flowerheads, particularly early in the season.

6. 'Madame Butterfly' (R. Thorp: 1958.) A dwarf type, compact, spreading, close-jointed, medium-stemmed habit, with a large mid-green butterfly-shaped marking in the centre of an otherwise silvery-white average-sized leaf. Short-to-medium flower stems are topped by smallish flowerheads of semi-double dark red florets.

It will exceed 8 in if required but is quite happy when grown as a dwarf. Despite the semi-double flowers it will also do well when planted outside.

BEDDING VARIETIES

1. 'Caroline Schmidt' ('Wilhelm Langguth'.) (From Germany: c1898.) A tall, erect, medium-stemmed, medium-to-long-jointed basic variety with medium-sized, round, silvery-green, zoned, wide-creamy-edged leaves. Medium-length flower stems carry medium-sized flowerheads of small, double, deep vermilion florets.

An excellent bedder, which (along with the following variety) has long been a favourite with parks departments in Britain for massed effect and also as a spot plant among green-leaved varieties. It rewards pinching-out occasionally.

2. 'Mrs Parker' (Parker: 1880.) An erect, slow-growing, branching, medium-stemmed and jointed basic type with medium-sized, silvery-green, slightly zoned, varying but broad creamy/white-edged leaves. Average-length flower stems support medium flowerheads of medium-sized, double, rose-pink florets.

3. 'Chelsea Gem' (Bull: 1880.) An erect but not too tall, medium-jointed and stemmed basic variety with average-sized, silvery-green, creamy-edged leaves. Medium-length flower stems support small-to-medium flowerheads not over-endowed with smallish, double, pale pink florets with a small white eye on the upper petals.

A good variety that will also produce a good pot plant, given reasonable attention. It has a tendency to elongate the stems once flowering commences but is more floriferous than the two preceding varieties and will accept occasional 'in-flower' stopping.

4. 'Frank Headley'—see page 213.

5. 'Rene Roue'—see page 214.

6. 'Mont Blanc'—see page 214.

7. 'Mrs Mappin'—see page 215.

8. 'A Happy Thought' (Lynes: 1877.) Erect, medium height, thin-stemmed, medium-to-long-jointed basic type with attractive large puckered leaves. The unusual leaf colourings are bright, dark to mid-green, with yellow-ivory central butterfly-shaped markings, edged by an irregular brown zone. The long-stemmed, medium-sized flowerhead is made up of small, single, crimson florets.

This variety has been included here as, along with its pink-flowered sport 'Pink Happy Thought', it is a popular bedding variety grown more for its foliage than its flowers, yet it does not fall easily into the ornamental-leaved sections offered to the panellists.

We have not seen a lot of breeding activity within this classification during recent times and possibly the hybridists are limited by the basic restrictions imposed by the genetics of such varieties. However, it is probable that 'one-off' varieties with some improvement or difference will be introduced.

Tricolour Zonals

Saving the best to the last has been a personal trait for most of my life but the fact that my favourite group of varieties is to be described so near the end of the book is coincidence rather than design. The origins of this group have been briefly discussed already and nothing can be added here as modern introductions are minimal and we cannot be sure that present names attach to the original varieties. Indeed, the natural depreciation or improvement created by poor or good stock selection can bring about quite noticeable changes in characteristics over a relatively short period.

These plants have no particular cultural requirements that do not apply to other zonals with a similar growing habit, except that where convenient they should be fed with a balanced (1:1:1) formulation to display the true and natural leaf colourings. While the flowers are welcome and quite attractive when present, they are almost insignificant compared with the foliage and are hardly worth encouraging with high-potash fertilizers as this also darkens the leaf colourings, and that is not generally an improvement.

A tricolour is so called because it has three distinct and separate leaf colours—one shade of green, one shade of another colour between gold and white and a reddish zone which overlies both colours. The overall effect is of four colours, as the depth of red changes as it passes over the green into the yellow, and as the amount and shape of green is inconsistent from one leaf to the next—no two leaves are identical. There are currently five different tricolour classifications, both basic and dwarf types having single and double/semi-double varieties, while the miniature types have only single-flowered varieties so far.

Panellists are asked for their selections in the same categories as the bicolours—separately as greenhouse plants but combined with bicolours for bedding purposes. If the bicolours are taken out of the bedding lists, however, the same ten varieties comprise the most popular tricolours in both sections, though not of course in the same order of popularity. The following descriptions are therefore in order of popularity for greenhouse cultivation, with their bedding 'rating' mentioned at the end.

1. 'Henry Cox' (First listing appears to be that of Turner in 1879, in which year this variety also gained an RHS First Class Certificate.) An erect, thin-stemmed, long-jointed basic habit, with perhaps the most beautiful leaf of any geranium. The golden-yellow broad margin and irregular pale-to-mid-green centre are both partially overlaid with a broad flame-red zone; the leaves are medium-to-large size, with gently rounded lobes and give a very round form. The medium-to-long flower stems support small blooms of small, single, salmon-pink florets. (Bedding—1st.)

May be found listed as above or prefixed 'Mr', 'Mrs' or even 'Mrs H'. There may be two distinct varieties as plants are often seen with a broader, darker zone and paler notched/serrated-edged petals. The latter seems inferior in all aspects and must therefore be recommended as ideal material for the compost heap, in the interests of future enthusiasts. It requires careful stopping and training to build up a well-shaped plant, which is best done over eighteen months, as it is not naturally self-branching. A must for every zonal geranium collection—the first choice of panellists every year the lists have been compiled.

2. 'Contrast' ('Merry Gardens' from USA, introduced to Britain 1970 by Gambles.) An erect, slow-growing, thin-stemmed, medium-jointed rather open, basic habit, with small-to-medium-sized leaves. The leaf is bright palish-yellow margined, mid-green centre, with both overlaid by a good red zone; the shape is more lobed than 'Cox'. A long thin flower stem sometimes has difficulty in supporting the fairly small flowerheads of small, single, scarlet flowers. (Bedding—3rd.)

The slow-growing, open habit also necessitates a longer growing period for specimen plants.

3. 'Dolly Vardon' (Morris: 1880.) A quite compact, medium-height, thin-stemmed, medium-to-short-jointed basic variety with very round, medium-sized leaves. The individual leaf is a greyish-green with an irregular-depth creamy-white border and darkly zoned with red which only occasionally catches the border, when it shows very brightly. The medium-sized flowerheads, of small, single, vermilion florets are well supported on a medium-length flower stem. (Bedding—2nd.)

This variety produces sideshoots more readily than most tricolours and forms a well-shaped plant, without excessive attention.

4. 'Miss Burdett Coutts' (Peter Grieve: 1869.) An erect, dwarf, robust, thin-stemmed, medium-jointed, branching habit with small brightly coloured leaves. The leaf itself is principally creamy-white with a small irregular splash of mid-green in the centre and overlaid with a medium-width, uniform, red zone. The small, single, vermilion florets are rather sparse, forming a small open flowerhead which even then can be too heavy for the long, thin flower stem. (Bedding—8th.)

Named after Angela Georgina Burdett (1814–1906), a leading philanthropist of her time. She was made a Baroness in 1871. A beautiful variety and the younger leaves are charming; indeed if it weren't for the smallness of the leaves and the wayward flowerheads (shooting off in all directions), it might have rivalled 'Cox'.

5. 'Golden Brilliantisima' (Cannell: 1910.) An almost identical growing habit to 'Contrast'. The leaf base colour is a much paler yellow however and the florets are double in an impressive deep crimson colour. (Bedding—6th.)

A very old variety that appeared to have been lost until rediscovered by Henry and Gladys Weller during their 1974 European geranium tour.

6. 'Mrs Strang' (Williams: about 1880.) A strong-growing, basic, medium-stemmed, medium-to-long-jointed, branching variety with medium-sized, lobed and colourful leaves. The leaf itself is predominantly mid-green with an irregular, bright yellow margin and orange-red zone. The medium-to-long flower stems hold the small-to-medium-sized truss erect. The small, double, florets are a dull vermilion in colour. (Bedding—5th.)

Perhaps the best growing habit of all those listed here and a good all-round variety, easy to grow and propagate.

7. 'Skies of Italy' Another strong-growing, basic medium-stemmed, medium-to-long-jointed variety with medium-sized, angular-lobed leaves. The colourful leaf is mid-green, variably edged yellow with a good, strong red zone. The small, single, vermilion florets form a full but small flowerhead on medium-length flower stems. (Bedding—10th.)

The origins of this one are a mystery, although it seems to have first appeared in the USA. It is sometimes alleged to be a single-flowered sport of 'Mrs Strang', sometimes an improved 'Mrs Pollock', sometimes the original 'Peter Grieve' renamed, and sometimes any one of three other older varieties rediscovered and renamed.

8. 'Sophie Dumaresque' (Eldred: 1866.) An upright, tallish, medium-stemmed, long-jointed, basic variety with large, rounded, colourful leaves. The individual leaf is very similar to 'Cox' with a broad, bright yellow margin and central irregular mid-green section, both heavily overlaid by a good, broad red zone. The small, single, shaded red florets form an open, medium-sized bloom on a long stem. (Bedding—9th.)

Stronger growing and with a red flower, but otherwise very

similar to 'Cox'. It welcomes a few extra months growing to build up the framework needed for a good specimen plant.

9. 'Lass o' Gowrie' (Grieve: 1860.) A short, compact, thin-to-medium-stemmed, medium-to-short-jointed, basic (just) habit with small, rounded-lobed leaves. The individual leaf is grey-green-centred and creamy-white-edged with a bright carmine-rose zone. The small single, scarlet florets form a small flowerhead on the medium-length stem. (Bedding—7th.)

The young leaves are as colourful as 'Miss Burdett Coutts' but the green colouring takes over as the leaves age. An easily grown plant that performs well in a $4\frac{1}{2}$ or 5 in pot but can be grown-on. Received an RHS First Class Certificate in 1860.

10. 'Mrs Pollock' (Grieve: 1858.) An erect, thin-stemmed, medium- to long-jointed, basic habit with medium-to-large, prominently lobed leaves. The leaf itself is mid-green with a fairly regular bright yellow edge. The scarlet zone overlies the green rather more than the yellow but is very attractive despite that. The long thin flower stems just support the medium-sized flowerheads of small, single, vermilion florets. (Bedding—4th.)

Peter Grieve's first introduction of a golden tricolour zonal that received an RHS First Class Certificate in 1861. A good bedding variety and holds its leaf colouring much better outdoors than under cover, where it fades too rapidly.

That then completes the descriptions of the panellists' most popular plants during the 1970s and it is no reflection on subsequent hybridists that the last mentioned is perhaps the oldest. It is, however, a tribute to Peter Grieve and his achievements in this field that three of his varieties remain so popular 130 years or so after their introduction. New tricolour varieties with improved growing habits (perhaps true dwarf characteristics) may be just around the corner, but such hopes have so far failed to be realized, other than the very occasional introduction to raise our hopes.

Cactus-flowered Zonals

This is the last specific classification that has not been separately discussed. These plants are not extensively grown today, although some specialist nurseries still offer a small selection; panellists have never indicated that a separate listing was necessary. Such varieties could, of course, be included in other zonal sections if panellists so wished.

Cactus-flowered (or poinsettia-flowered) varieties fall into three classifications—basic, green-leaved, cactus-flowered; dwarf, green-leaved, cactus-flowered; and an apparently 'one-off' dwarf, bicolour-leaved, cactus-flowered. The green-leaved types could, in fact, be further divided into single cactus-flowered and double/semi-double cactus-flowered, but while the whole group probably has no more than ten varieties currently available, this does seem to be carrying things too far; it would be better to drop the 'cactus' classification altogether and regard them as novelty single- and double-flowered varieties.

The distinction between these and other plants is the curling of the individual petals into quite tight quills, which gives a very unusual and (to some of us) pleasing effect to the flower-head. The double-flowered, including the bicolour 'Spitfire', are undoubtedly the most effective and, as even the basic types do not grow into really large plants, two or three varieties add considerable interest to a collection without taking up too much room or demanding any special cultural attention.

Stellar Zonals

Some growers would suggest that this type of zonal, which has been treated as a basic, green-leaved type for classification purposes, is distinct enough and has sufficient varieties to justify a separate classification. They are correct if 'cactus-flowered' is to warrant its own section. However, the latter is subdivided by tradition rather than necessity and, as suggested, may be better included in the more general groupings, along with other novelty developments such as 'stellar'. 'Rosette/rosebud' classifications are also traditional and equally unnecessary at this particular time and could easily be absorbed into the 'double-flowered' groupings, making the task of general classification a great deal simpler. 'Stellar'-type varieties must however justify a specific mention in any reasonably comprehensive modern book on geraniums; they are a development of our time, and whether or not they survive as a distinct type is immaterial today.

Mr E. (Ted) Both, of Sydney, Australia, must take the major credit for this grouping. They were initially known as 'Both's Staphs' or 'Staphs', from Mr Both's belief that *P. staphysagroides* crossed with normal zonals (P × hortorum) produced the 'Stellar' characteristics. It has been suggested that Mr Both's

P. staphysagroides was in fact 'Chinese Cactus' or 'Fiery Chief'; but in any case Mr Both left us fifty or so 'Stellar' varieties on his untimely death in 1963. Other hybridists, notably Miss Frances Hartsook of California, have continued the breeding in a smaller way. Although 'Stellars' were produced in a range of types, from miniature to basic and both single- and double-flowered, only about a dozen seem to have been listed in Britain and apparently only Beckwood Geraniums and Greybridge Geraniums are still offering them.

The distinctive features of this group are the star-shaped leaves (often zoned) and the unusual formation of the floret petals, the broad, lower ones being wedge-shaped and serrated, the upper petals being narrower and divided. The overall impression of the flowerhead is 'untidily attractive' and sometimes it has furled, cactus-flower-type petals.

The Ten Most Popular Geraniums

As described on page 149, the BEGS panellists are asked to select their favourite ten varieties from the most popular and widely grown varieties in the other specific lists—thus selecting a varied collection of geraniums, a list that should prove of value to any new geranium enthusiast who might like to explore the various types available before deciding for himself where to concentrate his interest.

Readers of this book can be given not only the benefit of these combined selections but also the aggregate selections made each year the lists have been produced. The resultant list includes three basic, double-flowered zonals (no single-flowered, although 'Kathleen Gamble' was 11th); two regals and one each from dwarf zonals, miniature zonals, tricolour zonals, ivy-leaved and scented types. Here they are in order of popularity:

1. 'Regina' (page 176).
2. 'Henry Cox' (page 217).
3. 'Aztec' (page 158).
4. 'Jane Eyre' (page 205).
5. 'Deacon Lilac Mist' (page 199).
6. 'Hazel Cherry' (page 159).
7. 'Highfield's Festival' (page 178).
8. 'L'Elegante' (page 171) and 'Mabel Grey' (page 154).
10. 'Burgenland Girl' (page 177).

The only confident prediction for the next few years is that 'Morval' (page 202) will establish a position in that list.

Acknowledgements

The further I progressed through this book the more I realized how much of it was an amalgamation of the opinions, writings, researches and experiences of others, all applied by myself, to be retained or discarded and so become my own experiences. So it must be for the reader, for the very nature of geraniums and their growers demands that some will disagree with the advice and suggestions, even the descriptions, that make up this book.

I have, of course, warned of the variations and exceptions that apply not only to geraniums but within particular environments and localities, and it may be that some of the suggestions I have made, whilst satisfactory in my particular circumstances, may present you with some difficulties. I can only stress that I am convinced that if I could manage to do everything I have suggested to every plant at the right and proper time, they would give me even more pleasure and satisfaction than they do already. I have also tried very hard to ensure the factual content is as accurate as possible—asking where I did not know or could find no authority for unconfirmed statements—and have learned a great deal myself in the process.

My real concern is not for my own reputation however but that I may have misrepresented or given insufficient credit to one or more of the geranium personalities of the period covered, whether by assumption, inadequate research or, more seriously, by omission. Geranium folk are, and always will be, more important than our favourite plants and the friendship and assistance (often unwitting) that I have been given over many years exceeds even the pleasure I have had from my plants. That is not to imply that they, and the plants, have not given me occasional moments of frustration when they have failed to react exactly as I had hoped—especially judges!

This book was to have been dedicated to the least frustrating person I know—Bette, my wife with all that entails, from cook to motivator, secretary, typist, greenhouse opener/closer, plant waterer and (most important) mum to Colin and Diana—at least I think those are their names! I must re-establish contact as soon as the acknowledgements are finished. But Bette would be embarrassed, and in any event may be more understanding than the hundreds of others I would love to thank for their various contributions. To mention everyone by name would be long and dangerous but a few 'group descriptions' should encompass everyone who has helped with this book or with my personal geranium enjoyment. So thanks go to:

The dozen or so who know they have given specific help with this book, which includes those who have provided photographs, of course; the many authors, contributors to journals, etc, and personal correspondents throughout the world who have unwittingly increased my enjoyment of the geranium— more ink to their pens!

My fellow exhibitors, especially those oldtimers (not necessarily geranium growers) who suffered this novice so willingly; long may they continue to grow even better plants, provided we have not entered the same class.

All the world's geranium hybridizers and/or nurserymen, without whom our hobby would become boring and difficult to sustain; more pollen to their brushes and pennies to their profits (assuming that they make some, which must be doubtful).

All geranium societies' officials and committee members, particularly their editors; special mention here of past and present committees and members of my local Merseyside & Southport Group and the North West Geranium Society (a BEGS region) who have, over many years, maintained a virtually unblemished spirit of co-operation and friendliness—despite my involvement.

Those unsung heroes, the show secretaries and their helpers, who collectively with their large and small shows bring horticulture to millions in Britain alone.

Last, and most certainly least, my fellow judges, whom I must remind that the expression 'you can't win' is intended to apply to them—not to my exhibits!

To those who have manfully struggled thus far may I offer one final piece of advice—*join a specialist geranium society* to improve your knowledge and enjoyment of your geraniums. In Britain we must hope that the two national societies live up to their fine objectives and begin a programme of co-operation—for the good of the geranium and their membership. In the meantime, prospective UK members must write to the secretaries for details and join the one that comes nearest to providing what you look for in a specialist society.

Index

227

228